CW00481096

# RULE

*of*

# JUSTICE

# RULE
*of*
# JUSTICE

An Exploration of Governance
and Social Order through the
Middle East and Asia

MB Abbasi

NOMAD
PUBLISHING

# The Rule of Justice
## An Exploration of Governance and Social Order through the Middle East and Asia

Published by Nomad Publishing in 2022
Email: info@nomad-publishing.com
www.nomad-publishng.com
ISBN 978-1-908531-45-2
© MB Abbasi 2022

CIP Data: A catalogue for this book is available from the British Library

## About the Author

**MB Abbasi** holds a master's degree in Economics from Forman Christian College, Lahore, and from there conducted his higher education at the Kennedy School of Government at Harvard with a further short course at Stanford University, California.

MB Abbasi is an economist and banker, and rose through the ranks in his home country to become the President of the National Bank of Pakistan. On his retirement from the bank, he entered the diplomatic service as Pakistan's Ambassador to Iran and subsequently Iraq.

After retirement, he studied Philosophy at the University of Toronto in Canada, and he has also been involved in charity projects, among other things, setting up the Shahida Abbasi School of Computer Science in Kordjii, Pakistan.

He is the author of an earlier book *'Capital Markets in Pakistan'*.

*Humanity will prosper in non-Muslim
countries with the Rule of Justice.
Humanity will not prosper in Muslim
countries with the Rule of Injustice*

Imam Ali ibn Abu Talib
AD (661–601)

# Contents

# AUTHOR'S FOREWORD

This book goes to press against the backdrop of America's recent ignominious withdrawal from Afghanistan. It is an event of drama and tragedy that has magnetised international attention, and it serves in many ways as an illustration of the very principles I set out to cover in these pages.

For Afghanistan, the event is cataclysmic. 300,000 Afghani soldiers, trained by NATO and supported by the best modern military combat training of the US army, waited no more than a few hours to betray the US on its final departure from Afghanistan. It has become clear that they had been doing nothing more than paying lip service to the US presence and had been, throughout, loyal to their own tribal lords. It is a subject I cover in some depth in my writings.

Ultimately, the betrayal of the US by Afghan forces was a reflection of the very low esteem in which US foreign policy has come to be held across the developing world. And at the root of this flawed foreign policy is the US betrayal of its own founding principles: the Rule of Justice. All that is impressive and world-leading in American life and practise, has been built upon recognising the prime importance of the Rule of Justice. And, on the flip side of that same coin, the collapse of America's reputation overseas is a reflection of a foreign policy that lost sight of these same principles.

Separately, Europe is once more – for the first time since the Second World War – facing the nightmare prospect of potential global nuclear stand-off as Russia's military forces conquer Ukraine and threaten to spill over to neighbours formerly enveloped in the Soviet Union. Diplomatic manoeuvring is in high gear at the highest levels. Time will tell, but it is to be hoped of course that better sense will prevail among world leaders, and that all are fully aware of the potential consequences if compromise is not reached. These threats, I argue, are erupting as a direct consequence of injustices rooted in society, most notably at the epicentre of the region under threat. Europe, still reeling from the impact of the dreaded pandemic, needs to avert yet more disastrous threats ahead.

This book explores in some depth the principles that underpin subjects such as these. I take no joy in the vindication of my arguments in what is playing out in world affairs today, but it is my sincere hope that we might collectively learn from the experience and, in time, build together a world that will be robust and thriving – a world that will be, in short, built upon the principles of the Rule of Justice.

MB Abbasi
March 2022

# INTRODUCTION

We consider here, how man controls his fellow man. Animals, it must be noted, do not control other animals. It is peculiar to man that he has become responsible for all types of tyranny on earth and seeks to dominate others around him. The revealed texts of the prophets have repeatedly warned us that we should not create problems here on Earth. Those who do so tend to claim that they are acting only as peacemakers. These sorts of people are seeking authority, and ultimately they seek to become dictators. But such tyranny is not confined to those who are operating in the state system. It occurs in every walk of life. In essence, Man – and it is generally Man rather than Woman – seeks to control everything within reach. He will control the women, children, servants, tribal underlings, and indeed everyone he can, always claiming that it is in the interests of creating a better life for all. The reality, however, is that he will have his own ulterior motives behind each act.

**Tyrant Leaders**

In the course of these misdemeanours, he will award to himself vainglorious titles: Emperor, King, President, Prime Minister, tribal chief, priest, and all that establishes his name as Lord over others.

Such figures tend ultimately, to meet a horrible end – humiliated, prosecuted and often murdered. There is some sort of divine cycle in process here. The history of mankind is full of stories of tyrants being brought to a terrible end. They frequently lead those around them to bring down spiritual leaders - prophets, saints and holy men. In such instances, where injustice has been brought to religious figures, the demise of the perpetrators tends to follow swiftly on the heels of their calumnies. History is full of examples of this. Probably the most famous is the crucifixion of Jesus Christ, who represented God here on earth. Today, his followers have made Christianity one of the great religions and people worship his memory, motivated to respond to the incredible gift of his own life which he offered with nothing in return. Jesus did not use his powers to kill his enemies, and nor did he seek to humiliate them. Instead, he sacrificed himself. It is a great lesson that truly divine powers are not used to kill one's enemies. Ultimately, Jesus emerged as the winner, and the kingdom which he created will last to the end of time.

**Treatment of the Prophets**

Another great martyr in this tradition is Hussain Ibn Ali – an extreme example of human sacrifice. But whereas Jesus had been killed by Romans (albeit acting under the influence of the Jews) Hussain was killed by his fellow Muslims. His death came just 50 years after the Prophet Muhammad had founded the new faith of Islam. This new faith recognised the Abrahamic prophets who had come before: Moses, Abraham, Yacoub.

All were acknowledged as prophets of God. But Mohammed was sent down to correct the misdirections which had crept into these previous religions, steering back followers who had strayed from the central path originally revealed to the earlier prophets.

The depth of the tragedy that befell Hussein is beyond comprehension. That those around him – mostly the first descendants of the original Companions of the Prophet – went so far as to remove Hussain's head alive, is hard to grasp. They went on to raise his head on spear and drive horses to run over his dead body. They butchered his family and all those who were near to him – the massacre of brothers, nephews, and even the 6-month child of Hussain. They seized all the female members of his family, young and old alike, and forced them, as prisoners, to walk in a human chain 2,000 miles from Kerbala (in modern-day Iraq) to Damascus (in modern Syria). Muslims were, thereafter, divided into two groups. One is the Shia who follow the prophet Muhammad through his progeny, Imam Ali Ibni Abu Talib, and his descendants. The other is the Sunni, who follow the prophet Muhammad through his companions. Today in the Middle East the majority in Iran and Iraq are followers of Imam Ali as Shia, and in other areas of the Middle East, the Sunni populations tend to be larger than Shia.

Tyranny lives on today. Even here in the 21st century, there are those who will crush any who stand in their way. Socrates' famous words still hold true: everything is changing in the world, but nothing changes the nature of man. A tyrant, seizing power and threatening dissenters with death, commits countless atrocities, and causes immense misery through jailing and killing those who stand up to him. Such tyranny can be through military rule or civilian rule, but always the most threatening tyrants are those who have not been elected, or who refuse to relinquish power. Imam Ali addresses this in his famous sermon 108 in Nahjul Balagh:

> *Nevertheless, now the wrong has set itself on its places and ignorance has ridden on its riding beasts. Unruliness has increased while the call for virtue is suppressed. Time has pounced upon like a devouring carnivore, and wrong is shouting like a camel after remaining silent. People have become brothers over ill-doings, have forsaken religion, are united in speaking lie but bear mutual hatred in the matter of truth.*
>
> *When such is the case, the son would be a source of anger (instead of coolness of the eye to parents) and rain the cause of heat, the wicked would abound and the virtuous would diminish. The people of this time would be wolves, its rulers beasts, the middle class men gluttons and the poor (almost) dead. Truth would go down, falsehood would overflow, affection would be claimed with tongues but people would be quarrelsome at heart. Adultery would be the key to lineage while chastity would be rare and Islam would be worn overturned like the skin.*

## Conflict through the Ages

Throughout history, there have been killings between rival communities across the world, generally triggered by greed or ego, or fighting over women. These communities have experienced this sort of conflict the world over, be they Christian, Muslim, Buddha or Hindi. These warriors have routinely crossed from town to town, and ultimately it is always the women of these communities who are worst hit. The womenfolk were subject to horrific atrocities, frequently raped by soldiers, left pregnant and with a whole trail of societal problems for their children in the years that follow.

The Second World War, for all that it caused so much suffering, led to a time when the world enjoyed a period of relative peace, during which time, there were checks on the usual marauding activities that had been common before. The United States played a major role in shaping the world through this era. Their intention was not simply to control the world, but to liberate society from the tyrannical culture of the traditional ruling classes. Slowly and gradually, the world has moved to a model where society tolerates less, the dominance of individuals trying to seize control. The US and a group of western countries have, to some extent, had some success in liberating woman, servants and children. The rest of the world is still held up by long-established notions inherited from ancient civilizations. Today, it is from the more liberated societies that changes and innovation have taken place. In the developing world, people may walk the pavements barefoot, but they carry in their hand a mobile phone that serves as an essential window into a whole world beyond. They may themselves travel by horse or camel, but they are aware of air travel. The West continues to develop, developing fresh innovations in every field.

The Rule of Justice is one single factor that holds value across all religions, all ethics and all morals. The universe is created by an uncreated Creator, whatever name is assigned, but all concur that the universe existed with its natural equilibrium on the basis of justice. It is unknown when the universe was created, but it clearly exists in its entire form with the sun rising to remove darkness at dawn and when it sets, dark returning. The world rotates, for good or for bad, following its circuit with the rise and fall within the solar system. Many nations, even empires, have, since the beginning of time, been destroyed and could never rise again. What is left of these ancient empires now is no more than ruins to be visited by tourists, come to view what befalls those ancient unjust rulers. The only way that sustainability can be achieved is through the rule of justice. Without it, they are consigned to the dustbin of history. Philosophers and archaeologists debate continuously trying to describe what took place in ancient times.

The tyrants rise and fall, watched by the media of their era. Great Napoleon Bonaparte, on his escape from prison, was portrayed in newspaper headlines: "The traitor Napoleon has escaped from jail." When Napoleon managed to return to France, trumpeting his success, a crown was placed on his head and the same newspaper wrote: "His Majesty Napoleon is sworn in as King of France." Such are the variations the world faces in its media.

## Ancient Philosophy

In 340 BC, before the major international faith systems that we now know had come into being, Plato led discussions to examine what was the nature of knowledge. His debate sweeping far and wide, with investigation that explored all the corners of knowledge up to that point, took the form of enlightened dialogues with fellow thinkers of the age. In the end, he came up with the now-famous concept of the Cave – now "Plato's Cave" to modern students. We look out from the dark recesses of the cave, and peer to the sunlight outside which is screened from us by a waterfall, through which we perceive only a distorted image. That light is "knowledge" or, alternatively, the very concept of "reality" but nobody can know it absolutely. We see only a version of it through the running water. Such is the nature of perception.

So no matter how much we may strain to build our faith systems on reasoned knowledge, and no matter how much we try to establish a structure built solely on empirical facts, discarding the flotsam and jetsam of hearsay and assumption, we are doomed to fail. We are doomed because we can never be fully acquainted with true knowledge.

**Unnecessary Conflict**

The killing of one person by another on the pretext that it is supported by some belief system will inevitably contradict some other belief system. All such systems are fallible, built on shaky foundations and resulting in a false premise created from unsound "knowledge." Tyranny leads such unsound thinkers to fall into the confusion of following such wrong assumptions. Islam, as a religion that is in line with the other previously revealed books and is the last in that line, does, however, offer a set of divinely assured values:

> *Surely, those who believe (in the Oneness of Allah, in His Messenger Muhammad and all that was revealed to him from Allah), those who are the Jews and the Sabeans and the Christians, – whosoever believed in Allah and the Last Day, and worked righteousness, on them shall be no fear, nor shall they grieve.*

Quran: 5:69

War between religions has no basis in good faith for all are ultimately human beings and are to be respected. Attempts to invade other countries and turn one's neighbours' beliefs against one other is generally driven by man's ego rather than any pious thinking. A good man, irrespective of his religion, caste or creed is always fundamentally good.

Islam further adds to it that all human beings are one community.

> *O you who have believed, be persistently standing firm for Allah, witnesses in justice, and do not let the hatred of a people prevent you from being just. Be just; that is nearer to righteousness. And fear Allah; indeed, Allah is Acquainted with what you do.*

Quran 5:8

Alexander the Great, who was driven to conquer the world, died young, having swiftly invaded a vast territory. Finally, the hand of death caught up with him in Persia while he was intent on invading countries in Asia. His words, now famous, lamented that no amount of mighty power, even the greatest armed forces, doctors, and priests could save him from the hands of death.

**True History**
The history of mankind has two sources: the religiously revealed sources and the scientists' discoveries. Drawing from the revealed sources, based on what is consistently presented in books of God, Torah, Bible and Quran, a narrative emerges. Those who follow these divinely revealed books are known as Peoples of Book. Followers of these books: Jews, Christians and Muslims. They bury their dead in the knowledge that they will be raised up again. Those who are not of the Book tend to cremate their dead. Among them are both the Buddha and Hindu communities, who together constitute almost half of the world's population. The followers of these faiths go further in submission to one another in a way that seems perhaps strange to the People of the Book. The followers of Buddha greet one another by almost kneeling down, while the Hindus greet one another by folding both hands, and their elders are to be greeted by touching one's hands on their feet. The People of the Book consider kneeling down and folding both hands as acts reserved only for the Creator.

> *"We decreed the Children of Israel that whosoever killeth a human being for other than manslaughter or corruption in the earth, it shall be as if he had killed all mankind, and whoso saveth the life of one, it shall be as if he had saved the life of all mankind. Our*

*messengers came unto them with clear proofs (of Allah's Sovereignty), but afterwards lo! many of them became prodigals in the earth."*

Quran 5:32

Killing and hanging are the acts of tyrants. History is full of stories of leaders who carry on their shoulders the killing of literally millions and millions of their fellow men, destroying heritage and razing empires. From here, the dawn of the history of empires emerges, each rising and falling, following hard on the heels of the one before. The Roman Empire, the Spanish Empire, the Ottoman Empire, the British Empire and so many more. All of these empires were ultimately washed away by their own criminality. War prisoners, both men and women, were treated horrendously – even an animal could not endure what these prisoners faced.

## The Fate of God's Messengers
God, all-powerful, all-mighty, repeatedly sent his messages to inform that in justice you prosper, and that any act that is unjust will cause suffering. God offered his knowledge to the countries where justice was practised in the affairs of people. But man is quick to forget once he is in power and has attained full strength. He obliges, everyone around him to kneel as a form of worship to him. The day is always awaiting – no matter how strong powerful empires he controls – when reckoning will come, and he can never escape the inevitable hand of death.

The Quran tells us: We send you Our messengers but you tarnished, prosecuted, jailed and even killed them. Like the Quran, the other revealed books similarly condemn tyranny.

The Quran also tells us:

The Rule of Justice

> *Allah has set a seal on their hearts and on their hearing; and on their eyes there is a covering, and for them awaits a mighty punishment.*

Quran Baqr: 1

And the Bible similarly:

> *Aware of their conversation, Jesus asked them, "Why are you debating about having no bread? Do you still not see or understand? Do you have such hard hearts? Having eyes, do you not see? And having ears, do you not hear?' And do you not remember?*

Bible – Mark 8:18

And the opening section of the Quran's Surat Al Baqarah continues:

> *And when it is said to them: 'Create not disorder on the earth,' they say: 'We are only promoters of peace.'*
> *Beware! It is surely they who create disorder, but they do not perceive it.*

Quran 2:12-13

## The War of the Worlds

European society led the world, through many decades, as a beacon of innovative thought. The age of empires brought conquering armies to take over vast swathes of the developing world. Local soldiers, fighting on horseback, could not sustain the war against the European guns, and so it was that the world was under the grip of Europeans for a period lasting nearly 400 years, from 1600 to 1945. They pronounced that their purpose in these invasions was to enlighten these areas with civilization. And indeed, there are some notable achievements, such as, for example, removing the monarchy from almost all Asian countries. The motivation behind this colonizing

22

drive was, indeed, to remove darkness from the benighted areas of the world. It succeeded in undermining ancient tribal ruling systems across the world – systems that had, until then, controlled 90% of the population, effectively rendering their populations into slavery. European rulers now gave them a new vision with new institutions and new infrastructure. The inhabitants of these countries were, however, understandably highly demoralized, and resented the foreigners who had invaded their lands and were now ruling them. Their struggles for independence were largely crushed – the methods of the European invaders were draconian, killing indiscriminately.

The great world wars that were ultimately to change the world order began at very the heart of the colonial control centres, right within Europe. Both the First and Second World Wars were fought primarily in Europe. White man was killing white man, European was killing European, and Christians were killing Christians. It was, some might say, an act of divine retribution from above. The war caused the death of many millions. Two other factors were also simultaneously to hit the Europeans. One was the Russian communist revolution and the other was Hitler's anti-Jewish carnage. History had not previously witnessed devastation on this scale. Almost every city in Europe was destroyed, and every family suffered hunger with the very real threat of being eradicated.

It was, some might say, a divine response to the evil excesses that had gone before – a natural turning of the circle of life, so that actions, good or bad, come back to their source in some other form. It might take the form of a pandemic, an earthquake or a war, but it lies in waiting and is inevitable.

The debate is whether, on balance, the colonial invasions also caused some good. If, as claimed, the invasions brought enlightenment or quashed some horrendous tyrant who had personalized his empire by frightening any who sought to rise up against him, then it might be argued that the colonialist invasion was a just cause. In reality, looking at Europe's colonial history, it is hard to justify such positive outcome from the invader's actions, and any benefit would be marginal at best. And, of course, to be credible in having a worthy goal, any such invaders would have to have left quickly once they have established and ordered system, and not linger to exploit their resources. Sadly, such was not the case.

## The US as a Superpower

At this point, the United States was not the major figure on the world stage that it has become today. The rise was only to occur in the wake of the First and Second World War. The US played a major role, both by saving the allies from the very real danger of ultimate defeat, and also giving Europe a new vision of life. The first thing was to decolonize and give all the colonies their independent sovereignty so that they could rule themselves. Most important among all preparations in this was to ensure that they might learn the methods of self-governance. In every step, it was vital to emphasize the rule of justice – that men and women would be liberated from any kind of control. People should be able to work with fair employment arrangements, with dignity to live life as they choose, and with provision for all to have houses, education and health facilities. People from the developing world are slowly inducted into such a model of society so that the poorer people are able to enjoy and learn the concepts of a new free way of living. Along with that comes the importance of them knowing the responsibilities of their rulers, and how their governance should operate so that everyone has their equal rights, and so that they are protected by laws.

One remarkable institution they have in the US is the Green Card lottery – a lottery for all where anyone can apply for the programme - ultimately for citizenship –  irrespective of cast and creed. No qualifications are required, and there are no checks on the individual's background. It is an open and egalitarian lottery system whereby the US invite people from all over the world, and accept them into the system, be they educated or uneducated, criminal or law-abiding, sick or well – all are welcomed with an open spirit.

Today, the US population, in its many millions, live free in the knowledge that they hold full political powers, and they can rise to any personal goal without restriction. In this system, they can prosper. President Reagan famously cherished these freedoms:

> *Freedom is never more than one generation away from extinction. We didn't pass it to our children in the bloodstream. It must be fought for, protected, and handed on for them to do the same.*

President Reagan

Europe also followed the same spirit, albeit with more cautious notes on the influx of new migrants. However, the rich Muslim countries mostly did not allow even their own Muslims living within their own boundaries the luxury of free citizenship. Foreigners who are born in countries such as Saudi Arabia, Iran and the UAE – and many other Muslim countries too – do not generally receive citizenship.

**Development Elsewhere**
The developing world has been given big leverage to develop their infrastructure and move forward to assimilate with the world community. They work to develop their education systems, civil society, and on top of that, democratic institutions. Initially, the US followed a policy that blended a version of democracy with centralised controlling authoritarianism,

deemed necessary in the face of the threat from communist regimes and the rapid spread of an ideology that was judged to pose a fundamental threat to the American way of life. On this basis, the US government felt it was justified in curbing some of their civil liberties in favour of the bigger picture and longer term security for their way of life.

Rule in the Middle East was, at the start of the 20$^{th}$ century, largely through monarchy systems, but Soviet Russian backed military dictators in opposition to the establishment leaders and succeeded in doing away with a large number of the rulers who had established military control in Iraq, Syria, Egypt and Algeria much of it under the ideology of the Ba'ath party.

**Rebuilding World Order**

The biggest task that the US faced after the Second World War was to establish control over the potentially rampant spread of communism. On this, they dispensed billions and billions, ultimately with the single goal of demolishing the Soviet Union, and finally after 45 years, Soviet Union. Nearly 26 counties, across both Europe and Central Asia were liberated as a result of the US strategies in this period and these nations announced their own independent sovereignty one after the other in the two decades following the end of the war. Many Muslim countries were previously largely shut off from the broader community of world nations – something that has changed utterly as these nations are now hubs of tourism and business.

Part of the US strategy was to create world institutions that would finance and guide developing countries. Among them were financial institutions such as the World Bank, the International Monetary Fund (IMF), the International Finance Corporation (the IFC, a sister to the World Bank) and other more general humanitarian organizations such as the World

Health Organization (WHO), the Food and Agriculture Organization (FAO), United Nations Children's Emergency Fund (UNICEF – part of the UN) and many more. In every field the task ahead was to make advancements towards a better life for the common man and woman. By dint of such international cooperation, curses such as smallpox, malaria, polio and so many other inherited diseases were almost removed.

As a result, a new international civil order was emerging – something that still harked back to the fundamental concepts Plato mapped out in *The Republic* to present his dream of the ideal society, tempered and adjusted to be in step with the societal norms of each nation. In this, the concept of Self is greatly reduced. All are to be honoured and recognised as human beings but the notion of Identity as a family, tribe or gang is to be played down. Even children's dependence on parents is to be reduced. As they grow up, children are to be given confidence in readiness for them to stand on their own two feet and survive on their own. Religion should be treated as some. thing private affairs of human life. State should not impose its own religion, and people should be free to practice religious rituals without any fear.

During this period, the US emerged as the "Leader of the Free World." Since 1945 it has made huge progress in terms of economic developments and also making enormous progress in computer science and technology. Every new vision of the world development seemed, through this period, to originate from the US, and was at root down to the importance it placed on the rule of justice. With copyright systems that favoured invention and rewarded initiative, the US increasingly elevated its world vision. The sky was literally no longer the limit – they reached the moon and set their sights on planet Mars. The world today is, as a result, a much better place. Few nations now dare to invade their neighbours. And, by and large, the innocent suffer less on account of religious beliefs, ethnic distinction, and other prejudices. The US sees itself as an international policeman trying to maintain the natural balance of the world through its standing and position.

## Enlightenment as the Road to Personal Freedom

And indeed, they have successfully liberated most under-developed countries from self-created chains that previously held them back. In the famous words of Rousseau, "Man is created free but has chained himself." These chains are ancient inhibitions that they have been carrying for no reason, but for all that they are mere illusion, leading us on a misguided path.

Or to quote the British poet, William Blake, writing about the miseries of 18th century London:

> In every cry of every Man,
> In every Infants cry of fear,
> In every voice: in every ban,
> The mind-forg'd manacles I hear

The "manacles" or Blake's poem are just such chains, and "mind-forg'd" captures the incredible power of the mind, shaping iron, even as it acts against itself.

## The Place of Religion in an Enlightened Society

Through all of this, there is still a place for tradition in religious rituals, and indeed this is a central part of all Abrahamic faiths. The US is not against Islam or Muslims or the practise of Islamic rituals. A Shia procession takes place on the streets New York on the 10th of Muharram each year. It is attended by the New York police who protect the participants as they walk along. Nor does US society have any objection when  a white American converts to Islam. You can open any number of mosques in the US, and there are no restrictions.

That said, US society resists the imposition of religion, or indeed any tribal thought system, on your children. It is not something that can be enforced in practice and clearly it is not universal. But the principle is there, and known to most – a fundamental part of the general American belief in the benefits of life is freedom and liberty. Whosoever chooses to deviate from the lifestyle of their forefathers must not be suffocated in their new life. Religions are to be adopted on the basis of personal free will. Indeed, God's biggest gift is Free Will. Islam, as the last region that God enacted through His messages via the prophet Muhammad, presents a religion that is ultimate - declared by God's last prophet.

Islamic society must present itself in such a way that all hatred of one's fellow man is removed. One of the great examples from the prophet Muhammad is when he pronounced forgiveness to his arch-enemy, Abu Sufyan, who had been responsible for countless wars and attacks against him, and who had made him migrate from Mecca to Medina. The Prophet said, in essence: "Today I remove hatred of man to man." Another such example is the famous letter of Imam Ali to Malik bin Ashtar: "You will rule two types of people: one who are your brothers in religion and the other who are your brothers in humanity."

## Early Dissent in Islam
Soon after the departure of the prophet, Muslims began to dissent among themselves, and they started retribution against one another. Muslims fought among themselves, the big disagreement being on the question of who was to be the successor to the prophet. The disagreement continued with Imam Ali, until they killed almost every male member of his family – dependents, young and old alike – in the battle of

Kerbala. Those who had earlier opposed the prophet in Mecca at the time of his initial pronouncement of Islam, came to power – initially Mu'awyia and Yazid, the sons of Abu Sufyan from Umayyad tribe. It is reported that Abu Sufyan actually never really gave up the pagan beliefs that first brought him into conflict with Muhammad. His children, when they managed to capture the throne of Islam, turned against the progeny of the prophet, and the Umayyad dynasty that they established did not carry through the original vision of the prophet.

Islam suffered heavily and created a bad name inside and outside the Islamic world. Tyranny became the rule of the game. And prophets companions were killed, tarnished and prosecuted. They turned the consensual Khalifa system of rule into a monarchy and tried to establish the Ummayad dynasty. It is fair to say that the Islamic way of life came to an end after the Battle of Kerbala. From here onward, the era of Islamic Empire begins, initially with Umayyad Empire (661–750 CE) and then continued with the Abbasid rule (750–1258 CE). These rulers terrorized every Muslim who opposed their policies. And those who accepted them as legitimate Islamic rulers were able to receive grand titles, medals and honours. Those who opposed them – and in particular those who recognised Imam Ali as the rightful leader of Islam – were prosecuted and hanged. The Shia followers of Imam Ali continued to suffer for 600 years through both the Umayyad and Abbasids period until the Mongol warriors, led by Halaku Khan, invaded and sacked Baghdad in 1258. The last Abbasid ruler was unceremoniously killed and the empire was ended.

All of this was a big step from the vision laid out by the prophet Muhammad's revelation at the outset. He took good care always to be a fine example to the community, presenting how best a leader should be.

## Establishing the Institutions

In time, tyranny returns again, whenever the opportunity presents itself. Only the US and the Western world has managed to establish solid institutional rule strong enough to weather such storms. It is only such rule of law which can check the progress of tyrants and punish misdemeanours. In such societies, there is no opportunity for anyone to grab power illegitimately. If, somehow, through the democratic process, a tyrant manages to come to power, he is soon enough identified as a tyrant and society turns against him, triggering the institutionalised democratic process that will remove him. There is no better example than recent American politics where President Trump was ousted by the Democratic popular vote. Behind the scenes, the nation's army was there to protect the democratic system. Credit goes to individuals as well, of course – Mick Mulvaney, US Chief of Staff, who came out openly to resist any abuse of the system, and who reminded any who doubted him that his oath was for the constitution and not for any individual man or woman.

These principles of equality have fed through to all parts of US society – universities, hospitals, charity houses.

## Economic Factors

Poverty is great evil in such systems and works its tentacles through the best-laid structures, undermining institutions as it goes. Western society has largely succeeded in giving dignity to all, and citizens are looked after with justice and equity. Unless and until people are liberated from poverty, they remain attached to their controlling headmen, following the time-established feudal system.

Islam seeks to place a great emphasis on equity and justice. The more you share your wealth, the more you will receive from providence down the road. How should wealth be shared? Spend on your near-poor relatives, neighbours, friends, community, countrymen and indeed anyone who is needy. Do not just donate leftover clothes or food; give the clothes which you wear yourself.

## Islam and the West
The 9/11 attacks on the US created a new era for Muslims and their relations with the US and Western Europe. On discovery of the event, most educated Muslims were, for quite some time, in a state of undiluted shock, unable to conceive who would do such a thing and to what purpose. The US, on investigation, laid all the blame on Muslims of the Wahabi sect who, it seems, had been planning this from Afghanistan under the guidance of Saudi born Osama bin Laden, following his defeat at the hands of the Russians there. Hillary Clinton spoke publicly about how misguided these plans had been, and decried the billions of dollars channelled by Wahabi movements into the propagation of anti-Western feeling.

The US and Western world mobilized a new hatred against Islam, and all Muslims from then onwards were tarred with the label of potential terrorist.

## Iran's Face Off to the World
The 1979 Islamic Revolution of Iran was unique among the revolutions of the 20th century and very unlike the communist revolutions of Russia and China. Here the revolution was led for the following 70 years by a leader – Ayatollah Khomeini – who had no ambition to create his own empire. It is nothing short of a miracle. The Shah of Iran had been an all-powerful king, supported by the two great superpowers, America and Russia, yet his demise was an eye-opener for all. As the Qur'an reminds us, old empires are destined to fade away when their tyrannical rule has crossed certain limits. The whole world

was watching Islamic Revolution carefully to see how Islam would fare in this new political upheaval. Unfortunately, evil forces played their role in detracting from the true spirit of the revolutionary path and the strayed from the examples set by the Prophet Muhammad. He, for example, had announced a general amnesty to all when he took control of Mecca, having earlier been forced to flee to Medina. Abu Sufyan, an arch-enemy of the prophet who had fought in all the wars against the prophet was not only forgiven for what he did to the prophet, but the prophet embraced him with an open heart and married him to his daughter just to ensure him that there is no ill will. At that time the prophet announced: Today I remove all hatred of man to man under my feet and all are brothers under the spirit of Oneness. Peace and forgiveness remain strong pillars of the prophet message.

Iran's behaviour in taking American diplomats hostage, as happened in Tehran with storming of the US embassy in January 1981, was certainly not the right course of action. Furthermore, the regime went on to kill millions of their own Iranian population, claiming punishment against those who had earlier worked with the old Shah of Iran.

On a more positive note, the regime went on to play a role in looking after Muslim issues in the world. Iran expended huge efforts, both physically and financially to save Palestinians from collapse.

The Islamic revolution of Iran had, much earlier, already segregated their community from the outside world, effectively becoming isolated. Iran took a strong stand on Palestinian issues and settlement programme in Israel, and they expended huge efforts, both physically and financially, to save Palestine from collapse. Iran forgot the lessons learnt years earlier by President Anwar Sadat of Egypt, and his humiliating immediate surrender defeat following their 1973 war with Israel – the

Yom Kippur War of 1973, also known as the Ramadan War. As a result, Egypt recognised Israel as a reality and accepted that Israel should be treated as effectively part of the US – ultimately a force that they could not hope to beat. This was the basis of the Egyptian surrender of 1973. Mindful of this, Iran's best option would have been to act through diplomatic channels instead of taking the egotistic route of confrontation. They caused huge annoyance without achieving anything from it. The Islamic Revolution of Iran also got further off track by killing their own population over the course of the senseless war with Iraq. Here they had clearly lost sight of the path of the Prophet Muhammad, whose act of forgiveness to Abu Sufyan and everyone who fought wars with him or forced him to leave Mecca, his birthplace, lives on as one of the marvellous acts of the prophet and something that should serve as a model to us today. This was a great opportunity for Iran to demonstrate the virtues of Islam to the world by forgiving, accepting and offering tolerance. The best way would have been to share wealth, culture and civilization with all the communities of the world. They could have opened their gates for all Muslims, directly or indirectly, through huge charity houses.

The Palestine issues could have been solved through goodwill and the careful attention to diplomatic channels. But, as a result, in part due of Iran's hostile attitude, the Palestinians have lost almost everything. Islam is a religion of compromises, offering peace through gestures of goodwill – the prophet's way. Iran's goal of leadership of Muslim world was not going to come from preaching alone; what was needed was investment in education, health and the other essential economic sectors. This would have demonstrated their goodwill in support of society's poor. Taking American diplomats hostage, as happened in Tehran with the storming of the US embassy in January 1981, was certainly not the right course of action.

Domestically, Iran's leadership claimed to be acting on religious grounds while simultaneously tightening governmental control on its own population. Severe regressive religious principles were enforced on day to day life. The Revolutionary Guards terrified the population, in particular the female population, who came under particular attack.

## The Arbitrary Justice of Traditionalist Societies

In contrast with the inward-looking repressive strategies of Iran's leadership, the US slowly moved forward with its target of liberating society from the many inhibitions which enslave human thought. Freedom of thought was crucial, and freedom of will was encouraged, even stimulated. This took the form of the young generation taking control of their own destiny and building a new future that was not dependent on parental approval.

Meanwhile, many traditionalist societies in the developing world were retrenching, almost moving back their resistance to the new international developments. In Canada, Star News carried a big news story that explained how Kamkhar Singh, a Sikh, killed his daughter on 8th August 2008 on the ground she was moving freely. He justified the murder by declaring it an "honour killing". In the court, he said that it was a tradition of his society that a father cannot tolerate his daughter moving freely.

In another example, again in Canada, a man originally from the Rawalpindi region of Pakistan, on 10th December 2007, killed his daughter together with the help of her brother and mother by locking her in her room and starving her to death.

Such honour killings are not, of course, confined to Muslim societies. All traditional societies where patriarchal rule is being followed tell the same tragic story. It is alarmingly commonplace in almost all the developing countries. And in many ways, this lack of enlightenment is a result of the national leadership which does are not allow them to develop society and which actively seek to keep their population in darkness. Some 60% or more of the world's population are living in suffocating traditional communities. This is the harsh reality of life in the underdeveloped societies of the world.

## Learning the Hard Way
In America, guns are made pretty freely available, and a license is not needed to buy a gun. Anybody can walk into a gun shop and buy a gun. There is very little government control. There have been several examples of people who have misused this freedom to commit massacres, killing randomly, just for fun. But still, the US government refuses to impose controls on ownership of guns. The idea is that people must on their own learn for themselves that they need to restrain themselves from such atrocities.

This thinking underpins the broader US foreign policy. The US took onto its own shoulders the humongous and overwhelming task of trying to liberate the world and establish a common way of life-based on free will and the rule of justice. As part of this, people are to be liberated from all manner of control, be it religious, ethnic, tribal, sectarian or the dreaded patriarchal control that causes so much suffering. The role of the government is to control crime, provide safety and security to all its citizen in equal measure and create better economic opportunities for the self-improvement of the people. In addition, it needs to provide better health facilities and educational institutions built on meritocracy. It needs to protect downtrodden populations and support them with special subsidies and a quota system to favour ethnic minorities. This is part of a model to ensure fair play between the conflicting communities. Internationally, they need to establish strong and peaceful relations with all the countries of the world in general, and neighbours in particular. And through all of this, make absolutely sure that people are living free of patriarchal controls.

In this way, the government is to control crime and for the rest it is up to the people themselves to judge good or bad, the relations one forms between families, tribes, and religions.

## Personal Ethics

Sin is another fundamental issue. What may work well in one society is judged very differently in another. Each society has its own definition of what sin is. The role of the state must be concerned only with controlling crime on the basis of principles that every sin is not a crime but every crime is sin. People would be accountable for their sins to their respective divine authority, and this is a different matter from the crimes society may punish them for.

## A Child's Birthright

Western society looks after its people from the cradle to the grave. Newborn children have, as their birthright, the support of their parents. But parents should not act as masters of the households; their role is to respectfully look after the family and ensure each member is treated as equal in all affairs. Children are not to be treated as slaves. No father should be allowed to mistreat his children. Tyranny is not confined only to ruler but indeed all those who live under a tyrant head of the family. Such controlling heads of family impose their own traditions, customs and religion and force it upon the members. In a world of freedom and liberty, however, children are encouraged to leave the parental home when they are ready so that they can survive by their own efforts. The parents can always be there in the background as support if needed. At the age of eighteen, the children move forward with their own lives. It may be that they do the humblest of first jobs, washing dishes for their daily bread, but at the end of the day, they generally succeed. From such roots, great scholars, reformers and philosophers have emerged through the ages, and they went on to lay the footprints of history.

In contrast, a life suffocated life under the influence of parents is very harmful. Parents in the developing world sometimes overburden their children, depending upon them to sustain a large family. Sometimes, desperate young men and women in this situation feel they have no option but to resort to crime in order to bring money to the family.

If grown-up children are enabled to support themselves by their own effort, the parents will ultimately face fewer problems and have fewer worries for their future.

## The Importance of a Constitution in upholding the Institutions

The US has taken part in a number of ill-advised foreign interventions – toppling governments in the developing world, leading to the leaders being imprisoned, sometimes hanged. Frequently they are charismatic figures, appearing dynamic and giving eloquent speeches, establishing a name as frontrunners for reform, and seeming empathetic to the humanity of the people. But underneath, most of them, once established, will only perpetuate their personal rule, creating a propaganda image of themselves as a heroic leader, while harshly oppressing any opponents.

The US fought the long Cold War with the Soviet Union on this issue – the fact that personal rule was not tolerable. It was their view that the cycle of government must be allowed to continue one after other so that space could be given to those who also want to run for leadership.

The recent US election with President Trump defeated in his bid to serve a second term was an eye-opener in this regard. The incumbent President Trump acted far beyond the permitted limits when he denied the election results, but institutions behind the scene correctly played their role and would not allow the country to waver from their written constitution. In this, the Commander-in-Chief of the US army appeared on television specifically to clear up the misconceptions that the army might be in support of Trump. He was dutiful, and made it clear that army generals take an oath to the constitution and not to individual leaders. The majority had voted for President Biden, turning a blind eye to the handicap of his great age (nearly 78 years), and confirming him as the next President of the US.

## Healthcare

The emergence of Covid-19, a deadly virus pandemic, threatened the world from working according to its established order. Many believe that it came as an act of God.

When a tyrant ruler threatens peaceful citizens for no reason other than his arrogance and aggression, then God will make suffer the whole nation responsible and indeed sometimes the whole world. Hence the unexpected diseases, wars and many economic depletion.

According to Islamic philosophy, a whole nation may suffer not because of tyrannical rule itself but because the people did not stand up against tyrant rulers. That is why the highest causalities of Covid-19 took place in the US and her allies. Covid-19 now melted away once the new President Biden had taken his oath of office.

The issue of healthcare does, of course, go far beyond this one big virus. In the poorer nations of the developing world where more than two-thirds of the population is living a life under permanent threat of illness, citizens face death everyday. When a child is born in downtrodden communities, they face mosquitoes, flies, and countless other insects all around them. The US and Western Europe have repeatedly invested huge resources to save innocent children from this unhygienic life. It is something they do out of civic responsibility and duty, but it stands in start contrast to the local rulers in such societies who generally live a luxurious lifestyle – an upper echelon of the rich which is remote from the bulk of society beneath them. It was the US-led initiative in early 1960s, soon after the Second World War, which succeeded in eradicating the deadly virus of small pox from the planet. To this day, the US spends heavily in Africa and other under developing countries to improve health facilities.

## The Model for A Modern Society

The modern world is moving towards a global system where public figures will be recognised on merit. An elected leader is one who is seen to be upright and honest in terms of piety, charity and integrity. Or indeed some one who is an innovator – creator of symbolic discoveries that are widely acclaimed.

There is a misunderstanding that modernity drags a society away from its traditional religious norms or ethical boundaries. But in reality, the major role of modernity is that it liberates the society to take their own decisions without any fear from any patriarchy. With the right leader, the society will flourish, and all parameters of justice begin from that premier – the head of state. More than 50% of the problems in a society can be set right if the ruler is upright, honest and God-fearing.

Such leaders will look after the poor people of the country instead of seeking to conquer neighbours and build empires. Their priority is to spend on the social sector and get children educated. They provide hygienic living conditions and bear fully the burden of those who suffer health problems. Likewise, industrialists must take responsibilities in urban areas. Western society has demonstrated what can be achieved through the charitable directing of private wealth to the betterment of the masses. They join the government initiatives and support them to spend on education and the health sector. The right leaders will direct carefully and with honesty, not for personal gain or cheap popularity but genuinely for the welfare of their society.

# CHAPTER I

# Justice is Divine

Justice is Divine. It is panacea for all evils. It is the magic. Without Justice human beings suffer from all kinds of ordeals – faced directly or indirectly but ultimately potentially impacting his nearest and dearest, be they family or friend. Sooner or later somebody will commit some injustice and snatch from others something that is not rightfully theirs. The victim will certainly suffer in a variety of ways.

No one can say definitively how our world should be governed – there is no definite answer – but what is a certainty is the vital role of justice and protecting the rights of others.

Divine good fortune descends on any society that succeeds in developing a civilization based on Justice. Through the history of philosophy, mankind has several attached this issue from different sources, be they "revealed" through a faith, or developed and argued following scientific evidence. The philosophers of ancient Greece devoted untiring efforts to establishing conceptual evidence to answer the big questions such as 'What is the purpose of creation?' Answer to such questions regarding a divine Creator generally conclude without establishing any great eternal truth.

Whatever the course, the arguments tend to lead to one answer: there is a creator. What is passed to us today from revealed faith, reaffirms the notion of a Creator. Among the most important message conveyed by the prophets is that this life is not the end of the story, and spirit of life lives on after mortal death, and – importantly – the life of the eternal spirit depends on earthly deeds. Among those deeds, honesty and justice are the fundamental pillars of all deeds.

That said, the exact nature of personal truth in religious thoughts is subjective. Indeed, it may not corroborate between the different religions of others. Throughout that, however, and across all platforms, Justice is a universal virtue. Justice needs to be recognised, followed and adopted as a final code of conduct for every citizen, irrespective of religious status.

All the prophets of the great Abrahamic faiths – Moses, Jesus and Muhammad – consistently reveal a very similar story and point us to believe in the Oneness of a divine being, and to ensure justice in our day to day lives. Those societies which live under the threat of injustice are threatened as a whole. To quote the bible:

*"Let him who is without sin cast the first stone,"*
(John 8:7).

The implication is that you can only cast blame if you are clearly yourself not involved in that crime.

Muslims, turning to the Qur'an, come to:

*We have created Man*
*In the best of moulds,*
*Then do We abase him,*

> *(To be) the lowest*
> *Of the low.*

Pickthal translation,
sura XCV, verses 3-4)

Here the lesson is those who believe in God will be successful and will do good deeds; the worst fate awaits those who lie in the judgement.

These are the Christian and Muslim indicators in the importance of the process of good governance. Every person is either looking after the work of others or is himself being looked after by supervisors. Every person has a duty to get things done with their fellow human beings honourably and honestly. No concessions are allowed, even for nearest and dearest or for someone who is considered socially superior. Each individual must stand by the personal contract that gets the job done honestly.

Justice and equality go hand in hand. A society can only survive and prosper when down-trodden people are taken care of. They need to be lifted up, protected from social atrocities and from natural hazards. Such catastrophe as the impact of changing climates must not be allowed to destroy them. If not equal in wealth, they must nonetheless be recognized equal as human beings, irrespective of cost, creed and religion. A fundamental truth must be that all human beings are created equal.

A surprisingly and well-recorded letter of Imam Ali ibn Abu Talib (AD 601-661), a successor of the Prophet Muhammad, addresses the Governor of Egypt as follows, "You are going to meet two types of people. The first are your brothers in terms of same religion. The second are your brothers in terms of humanity." This quotation summarises every aspect of humanity. In 7th century Egypt, Islam was still bringing new evidence to a wide range of people – pagans, Jews, Christians. This important letter to the governor of Egypt clearly spelt out the greeting that governance needed to maintain equality as brothers. The rule of justice is for all equally, irrespective of religious background. When considering the issues relevant to governance, the best governance is to ensure your subjects are all treated equally.

Tyranny and the rule of tyrants have had horrible consequences throughout human history. A tyrant generally has no religion and is driven only by his own ego. A tyrant is blind when he holds a knife in his hand. He declares himself God on earth. History has witnessed this countless times, terrorising their own subjects without fear of themselves being tortured.

Christianity holds Jesus as a victim of such tyranny. Pontius Pilate was the tyrant who, knowing the miracles of prophet Jesus – the raising of the dead from the grave, the restoration of sight to the blind, the curing from the worst diseases – yet was still intolerant and was unwilling to accept the evidence. Led by him, they crucified the prophet, a man with God's power on the earth. The path through life which Jesus brought with him was destroyed by tyrants. Jesus remains alive in the hearts of the masses to this day. But what Jesus wanted could not be implemented; the right path which Jesus wanted to show us was killed with his crucifixion.

Six centuries later, the prophet Muhammad came with the book of God, which recognises all the divine books that came before, and the divine prophets. His message was a continuation of previous messages, and the main emphasis remained that we must not create evil on earth. The oneness of God was an important point of emphasis in his message. God is not the father of single person, nor does he have any sons. The conceptual definition of God is beyond such earthly thinking, and ultimately beyond human intellect.

Muhammad's philosophy of Islam was cut off at Kerbala, just after 61 years, at the time the prophet Mohammad departed from this world. Hussain ibn Ali, grandson of the prophet from his daughter Fatima, was tortured and killed. His followers were also killed, one by one, each along with every male member of his family, under the orders of Yazid, the grandson of Abu Sufyan, who sat as Caliph on the throne of Islamic world.

Abu Sufyan was the chief of Mecca, and it was he who had initially led wars against the prophet's divine mission, Islam, and indeed it was he who had obliged Muhammad to leave his birth city, Mecca and migrate to Medina – a journey we know today as the Hijra. In a bizarre twist of history, it was to be Abu Sufyan's son who went on to seize power over the entire Islamic world. It was their mission to take full revenge on the family of the prophet at Kerbala. The way that the grandson of the prophet, Hussain ibn Ali, was tortured is beyond what one can imagine. One of the most heart-rending moments in the Kerbala tragedy is the account of how Hussain carried his sick child in his arms to battlefield, asking that the forces of Islam might give the dying child water, but one of the enemy soldiers fired a deadly arrow that hit the child in the neck, killing him. All the sons, nephews, brothers and brothers' sons, of Hussain were killed, and their dead bodies trampled beneath the horses' feet. The heads of the martyred soldiers were mounted on spears and taken to Syria, two thousand miles away under the heat of the sun. All females, old or young, were taken prisoner and made to travel the same two thousand-mile journey. Villagers en route were asked to throw stones and dust at female prisoners. When Zainab, sister of Hussain cried over the grave of her brother, her companions turned their heads low in shame, as stones and dust were thrown on their heads.

Separately, Jesus had passed through similar tortures at the hands of tyrant rulers. What lesson is learned from suchunbearable ordeal today? More than 50% of the world's population comprises Christians and Muslims who are raised on the story of human suffering at the hands of tyrants. God, all-powerful, all-mighty and all-knowing, did nothing, but allowed these tyrants with pride and ego, presenting themselves as gods on earth, to extend tyranny with full force, unopposed. God did not intervene. The reason was because God did not want to expand His religion by force or by killing. From this, we can see that God is merciful. In the Qur'an, the murder of one human being is as if you have killed the entirety of humanity. We need this system of free will and free struggle in order to establish the Rule of Justice, even at the expense of such torture and suffering.

Many centuries have elapsed since the deaths of Christ and Hussain, and the world has seen many ups and downs since. Millions and millions have been killed, their dead bodies thrown away without care. Empire after empire has risen, collapsed and risen again. Yet in the end, no tyrant has ever been able to establish success from invading countries.

Through the 17th century and onwards European powers swept through small countries all over the world to make them colonies under their direct rule. Europe, so advanced in literature, and philosophy, nonetheless sought – in addition to their commercial objectives – to open up the sleeping societies that lived under the rule of tyrants and to move the world forward, creating independent human life.

North America, discovered by Columbus, as history narrates, and subsequently visited by other travellers from Europe, was swiftly inhabited by newcomers desirous of this new virgin land with such enormous natural wealth and so much potential. They had no option but to kill the Red Indians who were not prepared to cooperate with European immigrants, and finally defeated them. It finally extended full battle against its colonial master, Britain, and gained independence in 1773. Today, the United States has emerged as the leading nation of the world.

Every day, the US is making further progress towards human independence, freedom and liberty. Wisely they place the judiciary at the top of their ruling culture. No one is allowed to escape from the laws of the land. Their evolution, over months and years has resulted in a structure where the US becomes stronger and stronger on the basis of liberty and freedom. There you can do what you like as long as that action does not encroach on the rights of others. It is a culture that has spread across the world, respected and imitated.

In the words of President Reagan in his farewell speech of January 1989:

> *"God has created America a little heaven on the earth between two oceans, Atlantic and Pacific, and asked the people of the world to come and join us and live here. It is a country of immigrants."*

In every field, the US started to work on with great spirit to ensure that their institutions, universities, medical centres, theatres, and indeed every field, must stand as number one in the world. As s result, US institutions have surpassed those of Europe in knowledge. One European country, France, was also forwarded-looking, and almost in same period when the US revolted against British rule, France went through a massive uprising against its aristocracy and the whole feudal system. For the rest of Europe, revolution was slow and silent over time without the same brutal damage to fellow citizens.

In the Second World War, Europe fell under serious threat from the German dictator, Adolf Hitler, who almost succeeded in demolishing the entire structure of the European system with his bombardments. The US played a big role in coming to Europe's rescue and separately brought reason to Japan by finally taking the drastic step of releasing nuclear bombs on two major cities. When the Japanese Emperor Hirohito finally surrendered before American General MacArthur, the US did not attempt to colonize Japan but did make sure to put in place safeguards against future recurrence of such disastrous adventures of war. This is where, following World War II, the US asked all the European countries to decolonize and give their subject nations independence and their own sovereignty. Europe wound down their tyrannical rule. The communist regimes also played a big role in getting Germany to stop any possible return to war. Hitler finally ended his life in Berlin, but not before Europe had gone through so many damaging experiences in the course of Second World War. Every inch of Europe was damaged as a consequence of the war. It was strange: white man was killing white man, Europeans were killing Europeans, Christians were killing Christians. Millions and millions of people died, and many more were left homeless.

But one must not forget that there is always a reason why man is faced by such suffering. It is always a reflection of man's own deeds. One factor in all this could possibly be that it came as an answer to what Europe had done to small countries across the world, killing millions upon millions, making them homeless and putting these countries under their colonial rule. It backfired in the course of Europe suffered as a result of what they had done to small countries. As a result, the history of mankind now begins, in some ways, after the Second World War.

## Will of God
In Justice lies the Will of God. Man and woman need to be liberated from all the various impositions upon them and live

freely and independently, doing whatever they like, so long as it does not adversely affect the interests of others. The law of the land is failing if it does not protect that spirit of liberty and freedom. It is wrong when these laws permit a society where some are superior, and where there are those who keep laws that subordinate people who matter and use the laws as they like in their own interests. The life of the subjugated suffers from being suppressed with a number of ways. There is not just the state organised control, but they are also controlled by their own self-created ethics and morality – something which has nothing to do with Divine Providence but can be born out of traditional tribal concepts which ultimately put lives in jeopardy. It is from there that people from some sections of society begin to be pushed backwards. Those in control perpetuate their own private influence at the cost of poor people, who risk being arrested under threat of being tortured and harassed. Those in control are frequently loved by their own progeny, who go on to erect empires for them. Surrounding the controlling class are vast throngs of hungry people, who work hard just to try and buy a loaf of bread from the meagre allowance they receive in return for the service they render. This is the scenario that exists in all third world countries. Slavery, not following the old-fashioned prisoner system, but imposed in a broader, more universal subjugation. The developing world has created large numbers of people – nearly 70% of the population – who live in semi-slavery. They live at the mercy of their feudal landlord or tribal chief. In a response to US pressure, a kind of de facto democracy has been created. The people's vote is under the influence of their landlords or tribal chiefs. Whoever rules – the living tribal man – is known as a Nobleman.

It is important to try and establish a set of definitions that distinguish these concepts on the basis of social systems. The "First World," then, comprises the US and the Western countries along with Australia and Japan. These countries have successfully made a breakthrough where men and women have been emancipated from all kinds of control, and they live freely wherever they want without any threat or insecurity. The state works for them, and every citizen is treated equally, poor or rich, in eyes of their governments - they are just citizens of the state. They are taken care of if they are homeless, health facilities are provided at their door, and every path to a successful life through education is made free. No one has the right to cheat or exploit anyone. If found guilty of a transgression, a due punishment will be applied. Lying is a big crime and is also treated sin. You cannot escape if you made your success based on lies or wrong statements.

In contrast, in the "Third Word" lies are common and simply part of natural heritage. People believe in cheating, deception, hypocrisy and in every aspect of life they will employ whatever makes them achieve success even through wrongdoing, and they get away with it safely. The entire command system of the government machinery supports these wrongdoings. This is the Third World, which covers all of Asia (except Japan), the entire Middle East, all of East Asia and South Asia. Something like 60–70% of people in these countries live in rural areas. They live at the mercy of local landlords or tribal chiefs. Their womenfolk are not safe from being the target of lust from ruling elites. If they raise their voice, they will be subject to torture and prosecution and will be jailed. A newborn child is faced with mosquitoes, lizards, flies, and many poisonous insects, as well as snakes and scorpions. Jobs go to the educated elite. These educated elites – even if they have exposure to the First World-systems from studying in the US or Europe – remain greedy inside and plot to devour the wealth of the nation. The ruling elites mostly come from rich tribal groups with a few elites coming from urban areas, surviving under their cover.

They exploit religion and make sure that the poor will always remain poor.

The "Second World" comprises mostly Eastern Europe, the states which were under the former Soviet Union. These countries missed the bus, because of having to live under the Soviet Union's systems. During that period, they were not allowed to mix with Western Europe as it was moving forward towards greater knowledge of life.

The only way to achieve success in life is to ensure Justice. If any country wants to become strong and rich, it must enforce the Rule of Justice. Even if only some 50% of Justice is implemented, the society will achieve something better. The most important thing in the Rule of Justice is to have an upright leader – someone who has come from the people, is honest and above board, with clear-headed thinking that focuses on the prosperity of the country as a single life goal. The ruler must not be someone who connivance behind the scenes – someone who appears outwardly good, but inside plays a malign power game and tries to hoodwink the nation. Plato in his range of many philosophical dialogues continues to emphasise that barren land will bear the fruit if you establish Rule of Justice. He emphasizes the importance of removing all temptations from the ruling elites to save them from being corrupt. His famous words still echo in the world: if your ruler is corrupt, he will corrupt the whole society.

> *"Of all the things of a man's soul which he has within him, justice is the greatest good and injustice the greatest evil."*
>
> Plato

The highest respect needs to be awarded to rulers or the ruling class because they are working as guardians of the land - they sacrifice their own plantations for the nation. Every plant they raise in the land is for all the people of the nation. The knowledge of the ruler is important, and the nation should never allow someone uneducated to be the ruler as he will undermine the whole nation's growth.

Western society, right from its earliest beginnings, had the motivation to search for surprises and try to discover the unknown. Ancient Greece was the first among various nation, though the Chinese, Hindu and Ancient Egyptian civilisations also tried to develop philosophical perceptions of how to run a state (although they perhaps persevered less, and left fewer written records). Greek philosophy is known as a cornerstone of wisdom. Even today, the modern world still teaches their books on wisdom, and they dominate the writings on the nature of philosophy. Their explanations are of great value when applied with care in assessing good and bad actions. Bad actions are sometimes necessary to achieve something good – the end can justify the means, as the saying goes. If the cause is good, bad action becomes justifiable – even undertaking wars, killing, and destroying land and property.

# CHAPTER II

# Tyranny

Through the ages, countless philosophers have set themselves to the study of what defines the Rule of Justice? Religious scholars derive their knowledge from texts that have been revealed to them by divine prophets, claiming the supreme authority of a truth directly consigned to them by God, the Almighty. The divine interdiction instructs humanity not to create mischief in earth, and forewarns that transgressions will not go unchecked. "Do justice," the instruction runs, "... and you will receive divine blessings." There is an eternal quest to hound those who have created mischief. "Do they not see what happened to the empires of tyrants, and the terrible end that meets tyrants, bringing them to horrible suffering?" Death is inevitable and inescapable, but the real implication of the afterlife is the suffering that will follow – a horrible and terrifying end, as divine will catches up in the end with those who have done wrong. The pages of history books are filled with the stories of the crimes committed by tyrants and how, in end, those tyrants are destroyed. The revelations brought to us in the chapters of the divine books show how the evildoer ever fails to see his end coming and is caught unaware at the moment of his destruction. Such perpetrators of wrongdoing misjudge the strength of the pillars of power, and fail to grasp that ultimately they will end subjugated.

The history of tyranny is as old as history of mankind. What befalls them as a result is only the inevitable result of what they have engaged in. Ever men want to control their fellow men through tricks and through threats, formulated and devised over the course of their personal evolution. Such tyrants, building a world view from their own misconceptions, start to consider themselves as god on earth. They try to give birth to a new religion, the devised from their own imagination. People often start to believe and follow them, seeing them as gods on the earth, but retribution will find a way, and they will be inflicted with some horrifying disease or other suffering, until finally, the community becomes conscious that those they perceived as gods were nothing of that nature.

Tyrants are octopus-like, many-tentacled. They conceive a multitude of schemes whose sole purpose is to seize power, and from there they seek to perpetuate the influence that they have gained by hook or by crook, pursuing their role through exploitation of the greedy psychology of the people. Their strengthening of their role as a tyrant, and their drive to consolidate control is conducted purely out of self-interest. Relentlessly, they devour the wealth of the nation, either through their friend and associates, or through those hired to do their bidding. One of the great tragedies of history is that we have not yet been able to rid ourselves of these mysterious tyrants. We know them as tribal chiefs and they exist right across the developing world. Such tribal chiefs want to keep their tribal community poor, enslaved under their yoke in the name of tribe. Their world is covered in shadow. Unfortunately, people persist in believing such tribal structures appear to be the best the form to live by and this form is even supported by misguided interpretations of religious scripture. Through all of this they do not realize what it is that makes them live such a downgraded life, deceived and anchored at the bottom of a class society, immovably the lowest of the low. This kind of tyrant is the most dangerous. To outward appearance all may be good, but the nations which come under this influence is doomed to destruction. Today, the world on one side has demonstrated the gains that can be achieved, creating man-made miracles, reaching up to the heavens with truly remarkable achievements, moving forward together and making enormous scientific and technological strides. Yet at the same time more then 50% of the population are living in the semi-dark ages, where people are trapped in bondage by traditional values. In cosy village communities, they can feel happy together for all that they are slaves to a tribal chief – typically the patriarchal head of a family or religious priest. They are seen as nobles of this tyrannical society and often behind their apparent humility is hidden greed, not thinking beyond their own family. Their governments collaborate with them, as they safeguard each other's interests. It is a kind of broad-based network which engulfs a huge area and brings it under their influence. The people in these communities are not prisoners in the literal sense of living in a jail – they move freely and undertake uninhibited their own independent business – but they are at the same time prisoners living in an open jail, and they are unable to perceive how they came to be in this situation. The nobles of these communities control the poor people both sociologically and in their political life. They create a class society, where seating arrangements are based on their proximity to the nobles. The rest of tribal group sit on the floor together with their own relatives. Happiness for them lies in managing to become close to their nobles. It is something that can only be achieved by those who help the nobles to keep everyone else under their control.

Such a leader was the Pharaoh Ramses II, ruling Egypt in the 14th century BCE. He made a large number of his subjects slaves, the majority being Hebrew. The leader of the Hebrews, Moses, was widely perceived to be a magician, and when some of the slaves came to the Pharaoh to betray their leader, offering to undermine his magic, they asked what they would receive if they succeeded against the Prophet Moses. The Pharaoh's answer was that would be given seats in his court and that they would be allowed to sit near to him. The culture of proximity to the tribal chief, and being elevated from their usual position sitting on the floor, holding a prestigious seat in tribal functions, lives on to this day.

Over a period of time, the system of tyrannical rule has evolved, emerging in a new form, the leader now defined as a tribal head, or 'noble.' This kind of tyrant terrifies his tribe and they contribute financially to him as tribal chief in order to make their lives easy and also to create a space for themselves near to him. In bygone times – indeed not really more than a few centuries ago – all palaces were constructed by the slaves for their tribal chiefs, who, in time, came to describe themselves as 'ruler' of a state. The newly formed 'state' would be formed from the clusters of people under their control. In the modern world, there has been a widespread collapse of ancient tribal state organisations – much has been destroyed, particularly, after Second World War – but their form still stands, now holding a different structure within the new overarching official state system. Asian communities – with the exception of Japan, which has surged forward and achieved first world status – are still struggling. Few have made good progress.

Third world tyranny is still engulfing communities in so many guises: ethnic tyranny, religious and sectarian tyranny, linguist tyranny, parochial tyranny and institutional tyranny. All these tyrannical behaviours are based on hatred to some community or other within the state. The set up of these small tyrannical groups often ultimately works against the unity of the state. Fortunate states are those whose structures and make up are based on their national background, and not built upon sociological structures for these always show signs of backwardness, and the growth of the society as a whole is greatly hindered by such smaller tyrannical groups. State organs in such countries end up divided. Far stronger are those states whose sociological make up is based on one cohesive linguistic and cultural background. If the government of any country is based on several diverse cultures or several diverse ethnicities, these countries invariably face trouble from within. Such disturbance emanates from that same cultural diversity, particularly when a country is not mature. Regionalised groups will continue to live with a selfish identity of their, perpetuating an internal power struggle within the broader nation state. No matter how genuinely broad-minded the leaders they have before them on their national political platforms, still the immaturity of common man blocks progress – they cannot see beyond their own personal survival needs and see no other course but to stay with their tribal leaders.

More killings, riots and political unrest follow, simply because of such tyrannical attitudes against the state, ever a battle to maintain status quo in the face of the state's conversion to a more evolved society. If state organs become part of this same tyrannical attitude, the system swallows up the weaker elements of society – those who live at the mercy of God, their voices suppressed. Those from among them who rise up to be their leaders, and who raise their voices in a call for rational justice are mostly killed, be it openly and officially or covertly according to how that particular tyrant may see the nation's historical background. Such tyrants do not hesitate to kill as many people as is necessary just to establish their personal success. The exception to this is the Islamic Revolution that followed the Second World War; in this case people at large stood behind their religious leaders. Otherwise, for the most part, people across the third world live still in semi-slavery – their leaders are killed and their political parties are destroyed.

An example is Egypt, where the people repeatedly made every effort to establish their own leader, only for thousands and thousands to be killed. People carried their dead bodies with remorse and sorrow, but, as usual, world leaders stood with the tyrant with whom they connived. Do strong tyrants serve the best interests of the world? Yes, we might say, if the world is to move ahead and progress it must not be impeded by emotion and sentiment. But, on the other hand, we are bound always to explore the compromised solution. As the saying goes, you can kill the snake but do not break your stick in the process. Maybe divine wisdom might have a scheme to destroy the tyrant once and for all, but in the meantime, there is nothing to be gained by drawing swords against one another.

The rule of patriarchs still hounds most traditional societies, particularly in South Asian countries. The most affected are women, who tend to be economically dependent and are reluctant to break with tradition as any change generally comes at a cost to them. Shalini, a well-known columnist, takes this one step further and declares the patriarchal system to be an organised crime. She urges that people should not be allowed to live under such tribal systems, and that they should rid themselves of such malice. She laments the tragedy of those women who cannot break but are obliged to compromise with a draconian tribal system that suppresses them. Across the developing world, communities are engulfed in this type of patriarchal system, and governments in power happily live with it, unquestioning. How can one expect such countries to prosper when their people are living sub-standard lives, surrounded by the most horrible unhygienic conditions. They continue to live in the ditch, never realising the crime that they are carrying on their shoulders, just for the happiness of tribal chiefs.

In the US and Western Europe, it is through their meticulous achievements that men and women have been liberated and as a consequence they the life they want, largely free. It is for them to choose the religion that they want to follow. From the positive attitude of the governments that control their day to day lives, they succeed as communities in achieving the highest level of living in the modern world. Meanwhile, the poor and deprived of the developing world live their lives frequently in jeopardy. Many flee to Western countries in search of a better life, dying en route in trucks and buses, or drowning at sea. The ordinary citizens of these Western societies come forward to adopt these immigrants with open hearts, sharing with them their own income - something they see as a simple service to humanity. They largely do not see the richness of the civil system they live in, or other related benefits that come with it; they welcome the refugee on their doorstep as simply another human being in need of help. Under European law, if any person lands on their territory seeking refuge, they need to be accommodated. Europe considers itself a land of peace, and this as one of its duties.

This is in stark contrast to the attitude of nations in the developing world. Even oil-rich countries do not want outsiders working and living in their countries. The children of these outsiders who are born there remain foreigners, without rights or any claim to nationality in the host country. If they conduct business in these wealthy countries, they can only do so in the name of a person native to the country, from some local tribal background, and that person then take nearly 50% of any income they generate. The status and dignity of non-citizens depend on the nature of the investment. Be they living there as a worker or working for themselves, they are not greeted with pleasure by the native population. Poor people from neighbouring countries are at the mercy of tyrant bosses, and mostly the work they take on is conducted as slave labour.

Meanwhile, Western countries give status to such immigrants, and offer them facility of having house and receiving unemployment benefits, free medical and free education. They and their children grow with confidence and they can join the ranks of the elite in that country, equal in respect. These first world nations, whose directions follow the principles of the Rule of Justice pass on success to their citizens. Of the immigrants create their own communities within the host – US and European, Chinese in Chinatowns, Arabs, Koreans, Iranians, Mexicans, and so on, happily they live in peace. They enjoy all the same rights as the nationals of the host nation, and some of them rise to become ministers, parliamentarians. There is nothing to hold them back from reaching the very highest levels of society. The individual is not defined by where he or she comes from or what religion they follow. These are simply human beings. They earn their qualifications on the basis of honesty. These immigrants frequently erect their own religious monuments and places of worship – buildings such as mosques, temples, synagogues and so on that all become part of the local landscape.

Most impressive among all of this is love for animals. These first world societies protect animals such as horses, dogs, cats, donkeys, cows, etc, and such animals are nurtured in hygienic open environments. In the developing world, animals are sometimes hung by their neck when being transported and suffer unimaginable cruelties. The silent dejection on their faces is awful to witness. Habitat is also treated with the same neglect: forests and green areas are destroyed in the interests of making money.

The developing world faces yet another form of tyranny. This comes from the institutions which control most day to day aspects of life. There are three institutionalised tyrannies: the political tyranny, the military tyranny and the bureaucratic. These groups form separate clusters and behave as if the world roared around their so-called intellectuals. If they do not form some kind of common bond through a union among themselves, then they oppose each other and fight for power. Political tyranny tries to subjugate their opponents by creating hurdles in their personal lives. The life of any opposition member becomes difficult unless they make some compromise with the ruling political power. The leading political party will try by hook and or by crook to seize the wealth of the nation. They know that without this wealth they will be squeezed out by one of the military or bureaucratic tyrants who lie ever in wait, looking for an opportunity to strike and claim a motive to take power. Political parties also try to suppress the strength of opposition parties through bureaucratic channels. They like to remove people from jobs if they have any involvement with their political opposition. They try to deny these people access to government facilities, such as health services, schools, drainage, roads, and they keep this pressure up until such people start to leave their leader and fall in line with the interests of the ruling party.

States operating in this way are a target of foreign intervention. Rival powers leverage control on the key individuals, pushing for strategies that will afford them success in the bid for global hegemony. The systems of government in the developing world were less of a problem during colonial rule. Even after the Second World War, as the countries under colonial rule achieve their independence, the institutions within continued to be relatively well-balanced. But slowly and surely, with the malicious changes widely unnoticed, these institutions began to increase their control, upsetting the established balance of society. Many countries fell prey to the caprices of military tyrants, who killed or prosecuted almost all the leaders who had struggled for independence from the colonial controllers. Through military tyranny, the balance of such societies was destroyed. I

World leaders found military dictatorships more congenial. They were more manageable – easier to control in the face of the new threat of communism. And indeed, for the citizens of most of the developing world, the concept of communism certainly held an attraction. Increasingly they began to support populist leaders who offered them social justice. It was a trap. People were being deceived in the name of social justice; ultimately, they would be locked into humble roles with a cap on their earning capability.

The world's leaders could see the challenges before them, and it seemed clear to them that if they allowed societies to become too liberal, they might be opening the gates to this new fashionable communism – something which seemed far more dangerous because it would ultimately destroy freedom and liberty. Indeed, the enforced systems of communism that the Soviets propagated during this period served only to turn the nation into an open prison, refusing permission for anyone to leave the country or for anyone from outside to come in and visit. If ever a citizen of the communist block gained access to the open free world they would be astounded by the new parallel reality – they had been so long closed in that they could not imagine breathing freely, and they marvelled at how beautiful the world actually looked outside. Even life in grinding poverty seemed far preferable to what they had come from. There is no substitute of freedom.

The Rule of Justice has at its heart liberty and freedom. What Plato was debating in the academy of philosophy in Greece in BC 350 was the light outside of the cave. Liberty and freedom are the real light of life. It is choice of every individual to live life the way he wants free from any form of fear. Men and women must step and abandon the false crutches provided by adherence to old taboos. The role of the state is to protect people from any kind of threat to its people, building vast avenues so that movements of the people are unhindered, travelling freely. The governing principles of a society must be based on serving the nation and to achieve this they need to give full attention to communications, road transport, air transport and rail transport. Such services need to be developed with state-subsidised rates in order to facilitate unhindered travel both domestically and leaving for overseas. Happily, technology today means that people can live and communicate with their loved ones without much difficulty. Modern communication interfaces such as WhatsApp enable people to unfettered access to distant friends and family. It is not something to be taken for granted, and indeed in the developing world apps such as WhatsApp are blocked by the rulers simply to protect the income and share price of local telephone operating companies. The Rule of Justice requires just the opposite: greater benefit must be given to the people. Imam Ai famous stated that humanity will prosper in non-Muslim countries if they have the rule of justice, and humanity will not proper in Muslim countries if they suffer from the rule of injustice.

Western countries have a troubled background, with a history of having invaded almost all Asian countries in leading up to the Second World War. They then suffered humiliation, mass killings, and mutual destruction across Europe. The

Asian world witnessed so-called "white men" at war killing other white men, Europeans fighting between themselves to kill other Europeans, and Christians fighting Christians. It could be seen, some might say, almost as a divine retribution for what they had inflicted on the world. Evil and tyranny had entered the heart of Europe. Separately, in the eastern reaches of the European continent, the communists' revolution also took heavy tool of the population.

Europe had been guilty of inflicting a huge injustice on the Asian countries, invading and occupying, unwelcomed. But it cannot be disputed that the also brought some benefits. For the first time, some kind of infrastructure was built thanks to these colonial rulers, and they brought also institutional developments – a method of structured governance rather than one-man rule. The education systems of these Asian countries were renewed and upgraded. Their educated elites, drawing a direct line to that era, today form an international community.

Since then has come the concept of the welfare state and Europe is now a leading model for the Rule of Justice. The divine cycle of accountability watches over it in its own way, and only took action when their leaders had displayed excess in their tyrannical rule of the colonies. Separately, the US played a positive role through this period of history. It was from the US that advice came to decolonize all the colonies that had been invaded. If there was a need to upgrade the countries of developing world and establish a better social and political life, it was first recognised from outside, rather than by the invading countries who were too closely involved. The US and Europe moved forward to prosperity again once they had settled down after the Second World War and decided to be rational, accommodating and tolerant, and sharing their innovations with all nations.

These nations strive, moreover, to prevent any other country placing their own citizens under threat, as often happens in cases of prejudice against a particular ethnicity or religious sectarian group. The US, in particular, and Europe in general, without ulterior motives, undertake massive efforts to combat the rule of tyrants, seeking to liberate the societies under them from authoritarian control. The model they promote is one where people may freely choose the way they want to live, and they are under no compulsion to follow the directions of their rulers as they relate to their private lives. The struggle against the Soviet Union was eye-opening example of this. It took nearly 50 years but they finally succeeded. Today the Soviet Union has ceased to exist and people have come out from beneath dark shadow it cast on day to day life.

In the developing world, the poor die without receiving medical treatment. In this, the tyrannical ruler depends on something akin to collective hypnotism, persuading them to accept their lives happily, living at the mercy of the leader. The German philosopher Hegel presents this in terms of the master-slave relationship. Blindly, the masses live happily in their foolishness. They feel obliged to collaborate with one another in a collective cult which affords them some kind of spiritual satisfaction, as if they have evolved their own rescue plan to find a way of living life under their master.

But there exists also slavery in its literal meaning, and this is just another part of the tyrannical system that exists in these countries. The slave is required not only to work for his master, but he will also have to contribute financially to the overall leader – the tribal head or so-called spiritual leaders – ultimate the patriarchy in whatever form it takes, controlling a large number of people under this unrelenting yoke. The masters of these slaves frequently have large forces at their disposal. They have the means to control their disciples through their own agents under them. These, in turn, are playing a double game; on the one hand it will appear as if they are a supporter of the disciple and on the other hand, they enjoy the confidence of their master. These people are nonetheless required to contribute to him from whatever savings they earn through their agricultural farming or other labour. In this they have no choice – it is a reality of they are to live in the community together in harmony. The burden of this unofficial extra financial contribution is something that they have to live with – an unavoidable obligation to their tribal leader, contributing to his already substantial wealth. It is a resource-based phenomenon, making their masters rich from the contribution that comes in from the workers beneath them in the tribe. Mostly such tyrant-ruled communities exist in areas far from the major cities - mainly in desert or mountains terrain. They operate far away from the routine day to day life of the cities.

What the young of these communities are deprived of most is education. Generation after generation, through multiple forefathers, they hear only one theme: that their life is protected by their masters, whom they must feed from own resources. It is in this area that the societies of the developing world face the deepest hypocrisy. Their elites stand as government officials or technocrats, publicly charged with supporting the community, but this is quite contrary to the self-serving actions they take in reality. The very smallest items. such as office pens, they plunder for themselves. They are robbers in the guise of officialdom, stealing office furniture, office carpets, and directing office workers to work at their private homes. Corruption runs through their very arteries. Everywhere, they can be found operating in this way, passing up opportunities for self-gain, leaving nothing to chance, every posing as ethical community leaders, but from within the system, indulging in the deepest possible corruption and enriching themselves at the expense of the community. Government facilities are compromised, fake medical bills issued, fake petrol bills submitted as expense - all is charged back to the government. Almost every elite, no matter what educational background they come from, or experience they may have from top multinational, employment, still at heart they are corrupt, waiting only for a chance to make money. It is this culture of corruption that destroys them. Almost everyone has a price, and the individual becomes a saleable commodity.

In this respect, the developing world ranks lowest of all communities in the world. They live at a great distance from the values of a good honest life, far from a disciplined way of life, and they ultimately have benefited nothing from the system handed down to them by their forefathers. This misery is effectively a societal disease, and even the spread of enlightened education sadly fails to cure these societal ills. Analysts, coming from outside to investigate these communities, invariably trace the root of the disease back to the rulers. Such behaviour goes back to ancient times when monarchy was the universal way to rule, and the leader would do nothing to nurture anything beyond their own four walls. Age after age this continued, through each successive generation, manifesting in one form or another, but ultimately unchanged in its essence – a system of slave labour where rulers never acknowledged what it is to be a human being. The slaves are not seen to have the same physical and intellectual properties as their rulers and are treated almost as another species.

It was slave labour that created the magnificent palaces Buddha, the great spiritual leader of Asia in BCE 500. As a young prince, with rule over an immense unattended terrain, he left suddenly one day horseback to go and ponder the meaning of life and the great questions that haunted him. What was it that people seemed to live such different lives? That some would be born to be poor or a slave and that this would perpetuate through, generation upon generation. Buddha came to the conclusion that there are no shortcuts: the only way to live an ethical life is to follow the Noble Eightfold Patch which he mapped out. These are:

1. *The Right View*
2. *The Right Intentions*
3. *The Right Speech*
4, *The Right Actions*
5, *The Right Livelihood,*
6, *The Right Efforts*
7, *The Right Mindfulness*
8, *The Right Concentrations (Samadhi).*

From within these Buddhist societies, Mao Zedong emerged in 20th century China, finally managing to demolish the long-revered theory of Confucius and raising a new society based on a plan for collective good. But the communist revolution itself was unable to survive long since any scheme of governance based on such extreme totalitarian control could not prosper and was ultimately doomed. So it was that the 20th century witnessed three big mass revolutions. The first two of these were based on the haves and the have nots. Both were communist revolutions: Russia's communist revolution in 1917, and China's revolution in the name of communism in 1949. Both these former communist regimes later struggled to keep pace with the speed of progress in the free world. The third 20th century revolution is the Islamic Revolution of Iran in 1979. This revolution now also struggles much as the other two did before it. The governments of the free world are creating hurdles for Iran, much as they created hurdles for the communist regimes of Russia and China.

The only major revolutions which can claim to have succeeded and which continue to perpetuate their influence are US Revolutionary War (1782) and French Revolution in 1789, both based on the principles of liberty and freedom. Their foundations are built on the importance of individual free will. Other Europeans countries followed suit and adopted liberty and freedom as their patterns of life, gradually achieving the same object without having to suffer the revolutionary method. As described, free will is something divine and essential. People need the liberty to decide what they want. It is for them to choose the religion they want. Society must keep alternative models of life on show so that everyone chooses what they adhere to, select and praise them and adopt them if their acts suggest a better life for everyone, with the ultimate goal of superior equity and justice. That is why western society tries to build houses that are often very alike, reducing the distinction between peoples. Those who have great wealth contribute to social services, making charitable donations to build huge universities, great hospitals and advanced programs so that people can be lifted from dark side of life.

The liberal interpretation of the Rule of Justice begins from the lower hierarchy. The weak have top priority, much like a traffic system where the pedestrian has first right of way. All other modes of traffic stop in order to allow the pedestrian to cross the road. In this way, houses are provided to those who are without shelter. Unemployment allowance is given to those without jobs. Children are given their freedoms, not under the harsh rules of overbearing fathers. Medical treatment and education are free. These laws are careful to favour the "have nots". The accused receives the benefits of the doubt. Large amounts of social housing provided by the state ultimately provide support for the weak and makes way for human development. Similarly, the police work for the people, always there to assist in any uncertain situation. There is no such thing as entitled nobility. Everyone holds equal rights.

Religious society needs likewise to follow the Rule of Justice and this places the community many steps ahead of where they would otherwise be. The government puts in place a system that shares the wealth of the rich with those who are poor and deprived. Refugees and asylum seekers are welcomed to their new home country. Society supports its week and looks out for those who are destitute. It serves everyone, without distinction of cost, colour or religion. Everyone is to be treated as family. As mentioned in Chapter One, this was a point that Imam Ali stressed to the governor of Egypt: "You are going to meet two types of people, one is your brother in religious terms and the other is your brothers in human terms." In this he meant: make sure you exercise Justice in all human decisions across the board, let people have easy access to you, create a society where people can adopt piety by themselves, not have it forced them.

The divine methodology laid out in the testaments of the great Abrahamic faiths direct people to undertake the struggle against tyrannical rule and tyrant society. Strike hard with resolute spirit, is the guidance. God will help those who help themselves. Even God's nominated prophets, for all their divine authority and the power to perform miracles, still have to struggle against all immense odds in order to achieve good. The Prophet Abraham had to face the tyrant King Nimrod; the Prophet Moses faced Pharaoh Ramses II, the Prophet Jesus faced the Roman King Herod and the Prophet Muhammad faced Abu Sufyan, chief of Umayyad tribe of Mecca. And they were prosecuted, tortured and jailed. From this, the only way to escape this ancient tradition of semi-slavery in the developing world is to strike hard against the particular tyrant who dominates their society. People living in downtrodden places should not be accepted as something that God destined them.

They are the victims of tyrannical rule that is human-inflicted, and they must simply struggle against it and corrected their path, whereby opportunities to become rich have been made easily accessible, and those who are deprived are being looked after by the state until they stand on their own.

Plato, writing in BC 350, placed an emphasis on the general aspects of being a fair ruler. In The Republic, arguing through a dialectic philosophical approach, he rated a society according to how upright the ruler could be judged to be, on the basis of which the nation would be blessed by God, and many natural treasures will become available. The most important thing is to identify the right kind of ruler. Plato preferred philosopher to rule, judging that the philosopher can direct society in a better way than if it were left to the uneducated. In such a society, virtue can develop, no one will hold a grudge against another, everyone will be materially protected, and no one is will be pushed down on the basis of poverty. The dignity of labour is another very important factor. All people to be respected equally and they should not discriminate against on the basis of wealth or status. No human being should ever be treated as a commodity for sale. Duties which are undertaken by the poor should be acknowledged, and their future duly taken care of. The western model for this is admirable: by law even the most humbled employees receive health insurance and pension contributions. They use all government facilities equally with dignity. The concept of personal servant does not exist. Those who are hired are engaged under a system based on laws that protect them.

The most important factor through all of this is that people at large should ultimately be happy. Their lives must be free from all kinds of malign influences. Influences – direct or indirect – that might place restricts on them or cause happiness to be suffocated, risk allowing society to revert back to the old systems of slavery. The only successful system that can survive and flourish for the longer term is one based on liberty and freedom.

The history of these sort of societies – successful in delivering the contentment of their citizens – is difficult to trace as records of personal well-being are not always clear and all is not always recorded. But the relatively short modern history of the United States is an eye opener in shedding light on this. In the past 300 – 400 years, pure virgin land has become inhibited by immigrants, mostly from Europe, gradually moving forward, one step at a time, to finally emerge as the world's largest economy with phenomenally strong fire-power. As charted by many historians, their first step was to rule themselves, as opposed to seeking to be a colonial power. The US collectively fought against the British empire and achieved independence in 1773. As quote George Washington on the importance of good governance:

> *"A primary object should be the education of our youth in the science of government. In a republic, what species of knowledge can be equally important? And what duty more pressing than communicating it to those who are to be the future guardians of the liberties of the country?"*

George Washington

Initially, they faced huge problems with indigenous owners of the land, known as the Indians, who were living a very simple way of life. European immigrants soon realised that the terrain was rich with natural resources and that the land could become the richest in the world, and indeed that is what finally happened. They tried to be partners with the Indians and work together but it was not a happy relationship. For their part, the Red Indian did not recognise the opportunities, and they continued to fight against the new immigrants. Ultimately, they forsook the benefit of the opportunities before them, simply because of their rigidity and their refusal to be converted to a new way of life. Most of them clung to their traditions and they remained addicted to living the way they always had before.

In many ways, the situation in the developing world today is the same. There is a kind of rigidity that holds whole nations of people back. Western societies launch a plethora of private non-government organizations (NGOs), designed to educate downtrodden societies and create awareness of new potentials. For the most part, they seem to fail – too often the local communities react against them, building barriers of propaganda in a quest to thwart their goals.

## Elections

The world bank reports that some 70% of people on the planet are living below the poverty line as defined by the world bank. Not only this, but they live in a state of semi-slavery, effectively tied to their landlords or to some other individual who controls their livelihood. When a child is born into these poverties ridden communities, the child is faced with mosquitoes and flies and grows up sitting in a miserable hut with no drainage. Generally, the conditions that they face are hideously unhygienic. What they eat is often near poisonous, and those few who live in rural areas will be lucky if they ever taste meat. For their whole societal system, they are at the mercy of their feudal lords who own the land on which they are living. Their livestock, poultry and other living animals are also likely to be taken away by local police, who themselves are underpaid and are obliged to make their living by snatching from those who are weaker. The great tragedy is that when political elections are held, these poor people are taken from their farms in trucks like animals and brought to the polling stations to take part in rigged elections. Many cannot even walk, but they are nonetheless forcibly dragged along to register their vote. During this election period of heightened excitement, poor men are bribed with as little as a bottle of Coca Cola, or with the luxury of mutton curry.

Some hope lies for the future in those who now raise their children to be politicians, and indeed some have received education from foreign countries to give them a stronger chance in this corrupted system. The reality is that they are up against firmly entrenched robbers and will need a lot to break the system. There are those in the patriarchal system who say that the whole voting system should be done away with, on the basis that these poor farmers cannot know what politics is and what they are supposed to be voting for. As a result of pressure from the likes of America, these essential voting rights have fortunately been maintained.

The political system is of immense importance – it is only through politics, and through political self-determination, that a rule of justice can be brought into practice. Under this system, the state must see everyone equal in the eyes of law, with an equal right to vote, and educated to a level where they can do so meaningfully.

## United States

The example of the United State shows what can be done by immigrants in a new state, starting from zero without any preconceptions or inhibitions. They identified that the basic Rule of Justice is to liberate the people from such strictures. With equality and freedom from humiliations, people can live with self-respect. In this struggle to establish a fair society, they founded a system where the ruler is elected for a limited period, his election free from any kind of external influence. How the individual runs his own election campaign is his own matter, as long it is not made through any form of election rigging. Those who acted honestly and followed their own objectives openly, would succeed. As part of this, it was made compulsory that elected candidates should not take part in other economic activities for personal gain – their duty now was no longer to themselves but to the sacred task of work for the happiness of the people. The success of the US model lies in this fundamental commitment to democracy. Their model, with an elected President holding a limited tenure in post and obliged to leave at a set date, is an example for others to follow. And indeed, no matter how popular the US president maybe, even if an angel, he is obliged to leave office when his term is completed.

The situation is quite different in the developing world. There, leaders consider themselves as essential and unmoveable. They create the idea that the country would not survive without them at the helm. This kind of attachment to power is a most terrifying disease and ultimately it retards the nation, preventing it from achieving something better. Former communist regimes have shown precisely this same refusal to leave office in time. In almost every third world country leaders never leave political office by themselves but have to be forced out – often killed.

Another important factor in the success of the US model is the principle of meritocracy. Across the developing world, much store is placed in pigeon-holding people according to cast, creed, religion or origin and many other distinctions exist which serve as a block to personal success. The US, however, created society based on the personal merit of the individual. A person's standing and success is based solely on their merit. In this meritocratic culture, any individual can reach the very highest job if his relevant merit is recognized and accepted. We have moved far from the days of black African slavery – a world-wide phenomenon that has slowly been dissolving over time. The crime of keeping a human being as slave based on their skin colour is something society works to clear up and consign to the history books. The children of former slaves can today increasingly live as accepted members of the wider community, without prejudice. Slowly but surely they are being assimilated into progressive societies. What a great success was achieved the day that one of their members became the US President, Commander-in-Chief of the Armed Forces, holding the highest political office in the land.

To some degree, it can be argued that Plato's theories on justice and equality have prevailed, and with them, the keys that will open the gates of heaven. Every day, the latest discoveries of science and innovation open new avenues for further exploration, with the result that the day to day life of citizens is ever-improving and they are living easier and happier lives. We can now see a way to a better life, unimaginable even as little as 50 years ago. The significance is that if you establish the Rule of Justice, barren lands will bear fruit. Western society, particularly the US, is exceedingly fortunate to be so rich in resources. They grow every kind of fruit and grain and benefit from huge surpluses of all. As a result, they feed many countries who are deficient in these basic nutritional requirements for their people. This is what Imam Ali, successor to the prophet Muhammad, foresaw in many sermons: humanity will prosper in non-Muslim countries with the rule of justice and humanity will not prosper in Muslim countries without it. With prosperity, society has flourished, and the pace of change has gone up a gear again, with new innovations following hard on the heels of even the most recent discoveries. Indeed, in the quest to reach the skies, scientists have finally reached even the moon, breaking the myth that there are limits that cannot be achieved. Their scientific discoveries continue, ever charting new vistas of the skies and finding the heavens filled will literally billions of new stars.

Every day new innovations emerge – fresh human miracles. Engineers shift the very rocks of the landscape, creating fresh passages under and over and round, diverting rivers and oceans. Witness the tunnel that joins Britain and France beneath the English Channel. Flying aeroplanes, once a concept the human mind could not deem possible, now criss-cross the skies carrying hundreds of passengers all together for thousands of miles. Now cars drive without drivers, drone planes fly without pilots. Cell phones replaced the old telephones that tethered us to the wall; now we not only walk and talk but also see friends and relatives live on the screen. Completely inconceivable to a previous generation. Such miracles of development have not appeared simply by themselves. There exists a divine blessing for those societies which have upgraded the way they approach the universe. President Reagan of America once described the US as a little heaven on the deck of this earth, lying between two oceans – Atlantic and Pacific – and he invited people of the world to come and live here. It is a country made by immigrants and for immigrants. There they can live happily together, irrespective of cast, creed, religious sect, race, ethnic grouping and linguistic roots.

The German philosopher Hegel (1770–1831) predicted the importance we would all place on the quest for knowledge and science:

*Not curiosity, not vanity, not the consideration of expediency, not duty and conscientiousness, but an unquenchable, unhappy thirst that brooks no compromise leads us to truth.*

Hegel - *Schrieb's zum Andenken*

The philosophers of the Enlightenment pointed to the divine right of reasoned logic, as against self-created notions of faith. In such rationalism, there is a divinity that has authority to serve as the essential guide for government.

The US's adherence to these teachings of the Enlightenment has given them a fair and practical Democracy. These teachings they have adopted honestly, and they follow them inch by inch in the spirit of an honest and dedicated government. The presidents respect their legal term and dutifully hand on to the next, knowing fully what stability and prosperity means for the country, and the need for all to work in a coordinated fashion, moving in one direction. Today, the United States surpasses the European countries in almost every field. They involve their citizens in all academic disciplines and all walks of public life, and these things all create a sense of spirit, making the US a great nation. The country is home to a large number of the most intellectual seats of learning in the world. The elite universities of the Ivy league are comparable to ancient establishments of learning such as Cambridge and Oxford universities in the UK; and American technology has become established as world-leading. Ultimately, it was the intervention of the US that saved Europe from collapse as they struggled to beat off the attacks from Hitler in the Second World War. And the US was the first country to discover the atom bomb, as demonstrated when it was used against Japan. Once the Japanese forces realised the impact that the atom bomb had had, with the immense casualties that had resulted, they had no option but to surrender. The world had been under threat of being completely destroyed and the US action was wise in averting further destruction.

Having conquered Japan, the US did not then make it a colony – such a step would have been against US principles. They themselves had been on the receiving end of the colony experience, as a colony of the British, and they therefore did not want to do same thing that they had themselves opposed so vehemently. This decision was based on the conviction that it is best to stay rational and honest and not to create a lingering threat to a nation they had defeated. Rule with honesty bears dividends. It pays much better than when one exploits the weaker side. The Rule of Justice must protect every race and ethnicity, or any other minorities that are under state-organised threat. Ultimately, God blesses those whose conduct is honest and who does not have evil eyes on the resources of those who are weaker.

The success that has been enjoyed by the First World lies in having stuck to its own reform programmes, without aid or external support. They decided to demolish the fake walls that had been constructed around their notional empires. Their only solution was to establish the Rule of Justice. The pillar of Rule of Justice is to liberate society from inhibitions, and from wrongly adopting beliefs without proper background knowledge.

## Faith in a Rational Society

Such liberty and freedom do not need to come at the expense of respect for religious practises. People should remain free to adopt the religion that they chose, without having obligations imposed upon them. There is, for many, an inner truth that God is the only creator and one must worship Him alone, confident in the knowledge that it is he who created the universe, and that everything in it belongs to him, and nothing moves – even the autumn leaves dropping from the trees – without his knowledge. This does not stop human beings acquiring a deeper knowledge of their universe. Seeking to know and investigate his creation is not something that is against the creator. Everyone has the right to choose the way he wants to worship. If someone is not worshipping, it is for him to win or lose in life, and for him alone. No other commentator has the right to judge some other worshipper. God has created human beings and given them free will so it is for them to decide what is right and what is not right.

A society is created by self-imposed disciplines. In the US there is no control on buying and selling guns freely. People realise that killing another innocent person is not good and that is a more powerful deterrent than a government attempting to bring in a licence on holding guns. Societies which have gun control systems face more crime than societies freely living without controls.

Under the Rule of Justice, laws must rule, and no one should feel they are above law, but, at the same time, state authorities must not force people to live the way they want to live. Self-imposed discipline is a more effective controller of human action.

**General**

Societies cannot prosper if they keep large populations under threat, subject to suppression and humiliation. All other efforts will go in waste, no matter how vigorously followed, if there is such injustice. Prosperity lies in the happiness of the masses.

The real-world models of life followed in US and Western society have certainly had their ups and downs through time as they evolved, but they have corrected elements that went wrong and put systems in place to ensure they do not repeat. The values of liberal democracy have been key in their success. It does not matter if an elected President worked as a saint, he must still go as soon as his tenure has reached its term. In the developing world everyone wants power, and everyone wants to be dictator. When they finally refuse to yield their position of power, they end up being pushed and frequently killed. It has become a routine game in the politics of these countries.

The most important aspect of the Rule of Justice is its implementation by the leaders who rule the country. The Greeks and Romans, now nearly 3,000 years ago, came to the conclusion that no one should have absolute authority to rule. The great thinkers of ancient Greek philosophy, most notably Plato in his Republic, was a proponent of philosophical rule on the basis that philosophers have, through study, gained an in-depth understanding of human behaviour, and can assign jobs better than those who are uneducated. The ruler's background, then, has a profound effect on the nation. If the ruler is corrupt, he will ultimately corrupt the whole society. The trickle-down effect begins from the top and runs down, permeating all. Reforms, on the other hand, begin from the bottom as the society pushes for revolutionary measures. The ancient Romans decided that there should be two people in collaboration together in order to achieve balanced rule. These were the check and the balance, providing a route of success. The Roman leader Caesar was killed on the steps of the senate in 44 AD simply because he had declared himself King of Rome and refused to accept the end of his term of rule. The tyrannical rule of dictators is particularly evil when you look to its long-term consequences. Always, consensus will be a better way to run a nation's governance, and that is the only way to achieve a balanced system that can operate fairly for public good.

# CHAPTER III

# The Treason of the Intellectual

What is right and what is wrong is something that needs to be visualized with a calm reflective eye, free of fear or any personal bias. It is a bias that none of us can confidently declare ourselves to be wholly free of. How much are we each indoctrinated, by whatever privilege we may carry? Or blinded by the acceptance of whatever birthrights we came into the world with? And how much has ego distorted our life's path?

To answer these questions, we need to look to our past. Each era of history has its own unique character. Ours, today, is the world that was shaped following the upheavals of the Second World War. Caught between the twin polarities of the US and Russian visions for a new world order, we find ourselves determining our own middle way. But both are an intrinsic part of who we are, and have played enormous roles in shaping our world's geography. It is they who have drawn the map of the contemporary world we inhabit, and to move forward in that world is to know how those polarities interplay the one with the other. Our great thinkers and philosophers peer into the future to discern what lies ahead – to see what may be harmful and to protect ourselves within the global ambitions of these great forces.

The Second World War was won by the allied forces with the support of the US. Hitler and his allies were vanquished. The fate of Europe, the Middle East, Asia and Africa now all lies in the hands of those victors. For her part, the Soviet Union managed to seize what had fallen under her control. The Western Allies decided – with some reluctance – to restore their erstwhile colonies to their position of sovereign independence. Wherever they could, they used their foresight to draw up a new map of their choice, effectively establishing the dominion of each nation, bestowing its new place of honour and placing new rulers.

The US wanted to maintain some balance in this new world order and protect the new nations by encouraging each to have its own system of governance based on the rights of common men. The Soviet communist party offered a solution that was very popular among common the poor, who were enthusiastic about demolishing the rich man's empire that had oppressed them so long, and establishing in its place a communist rule. The US initially wanted to demonstrate that democratic rule would bring these new sovereign nations a shiny new future, but they were also wary that the popular vote would encourage socialist groups to win the elections. For this reason, the US preferred to facilitate the rise to power of a new generation of military dictators. Such was the fate that befell Turkey, Indonesia, Pakistan, Algeria, and so many other countries. The popular leaders of these countries, who had been trained in democratic rules of governance as part of their struggle against imperial colonial rule, now wanted to take a leadership role in the new nations. The populist potential leaders – products of the historical struggle against colonial rule were found themselves sidetracked and in danger of endorsing some either authoritarian ruler or falling into some communist style of one - party rule. Some of these leaders were prosecuted and jailed, others simply killed. It was a struggle that generally ended badly for the freedom fighters, and military rule was imposed in most of the new sovereign states. The new military leaders were protected by the West and patronized with lots of financial support.

The first generation after the Second World War had no experience of leadership other than seeing men in military uniform as the head of government. They learned to be subordinate to military dictatorship. School children and intellectuals lived in the agony of pretending not to know the basic philosophy of politics. Those who were well educated could not follow their own ambitions to join the government systems of their homelands. They had always ultimately to bow to the will of a man who held a gun in his hand.

This was particularly true in South America, Asia, and Africa. The population learnt through generation upon generation that their world was infected by the disease of hypocrisy, deceit, lies and corruption. Every act that could make them breathe free was controlled by those who walked in the corridors of power. Democracy, trumpeted by the US, was little more than a distant slogan for these peoples.

The debate surrounding much of this was whether the end might justify the means – whether the plan for a potential democracy of the future would justify draconian crackdowns on liberty in the meantime. Was there some middle ground of compromise for the superpowers in this period? Could the essential principles of justice be waived? And how should we handle those populist leaders who had support that might be judged broadly "democratic" even though it was clear that the personalities involved were likely to ultimately emerge as despots. The debate still rumbles on. It is not easy task to assess how the world might have emerged if such leaders had succeeded – Ahmed Ben Bella of Algeria, Mohammad Mosaddegh of Iran, Adnan Menderes of Turkey, Sukarno of Indonesia, Bhutto of Pakistan, Mohammed Morsi of Egypt. These and so on many others with similar backgrounds were eliminated from their nation's democratic process on the basis of some assessment of a long term of "good" that would serve the country better.

The thinking community in the US was in constant debate on this subject. They adjusted their ethical boundaries, kept blaming leaders who seemed to lack the resilience to stand on their own, and stood by to watch the killing of vast numbers of civilians across the developing world. An example is the more than 20,000 people killed in Egypt in the process of the military dictator firming up his authority and eliminating any potential opponents in the land. The Egyptian Army General quickly held a fake democratic vote for himself and he was swiftly recognized by every interested party in the western world. World leaders who were prominent champions of justice cast aside all responsibilities and rewarded General Sissi with the showcase of a true and real democracy. This lamentable reality of the high treason of the world's intellectuals. Sisi's erstwhile President elect, Mohammed Morsi, went on to suffer a court judgement that was a foregone conclusion and died in prison. This is an example of the great gulf that lies between the "truth" presented by the propaganda machines of the world's big powers, and the contrasting falsehood of the way they operate.

Such mixing of truth and falsehood is perilous, of course. All the revealed books emphasise the dangers. Yet there were no voices raised high from the world's great international thinkers, statesmen or scholars when it came to the daylight political robbery that took place in Egypt. Their quiet argument, expressed only mutedly between themselves, is that will be that short term evil must be supported to achieve the longer term goal of good. Therefore we must adjust our evaluation of what is good or moral and build in a separate factor: that which is necessary and can save us from bigger disasters.

Failed popular leaders such as Morsi are followed by a more canny operator, generally supported by external forces, and frequently propelling the nation to war as part of this. With nationalist sentiments stirred, they can summon fresh popular support, entrench their personal rule, establish a cult like aura around their name all the time and then move to create a dynasty. Democratic rule, by contrast, has to be time-bound. Come what may, no matter how perfect may be the leader, he or she must depart political office as soon tenure is completed.

One of the main problems for government, particularly faced in the Muslim world where – and may the reader please forgive the generalisation born of personal experience – life is arguably more influenced by emotions and sentiments, is that the voting public is not as alert as they should be to the potential shadow ahead. They express the consensus of popular vote, but take lightly the leader's subsequent adherence to the limited tenure of rule. When the time comes, the leader will need to accept losing and retire from the political arena, giving others their chance to play their role and implement a different set of ideas. This is something that is enshrined and deeply respected in the US and Western Europe. Their leaders are constrained by checks and balances, and this reduces the opportunity for self-serving popularity to their personal advantage. The system is designed to favour collective achievement and the broader benefit of all. Once they have left office, there is a limited amount that they can do to hold their good work to their political advantage. In start contrast, the system in the developing world favours leaders who create their own dominion, as if they are the beginning and end of the nation's leadership and the only option available. The bulk of the population here – the subsistence-living masses – are effectively slaves for humble jobs, for bread to feed themselves, for basics such as drinking water, for better hygienic conditions, for security from political robbery, for better medical services, and finally furtive in resistance to the police, to others who rob them, and ultimately to robbers themselves. Unless and until these societies can make serious reforms towards these fundamentals issues, the developing world will be unable to rid itself from its these long-entrenched ordeals.

The Soviet Union, in its battle against the US to control the world order actively and unhesitatingly motivated its interests allied to communism and set up military coups across the Middle East and Central Asia. For the Middle East, several were in the name of Ba'ath party. The established monarchs were killed. Across Iraq, Syria and Egypt they were replaced with army generals. The US, facing the loss of its command centres, did what it could to restore some balance through the other army generals.

The next era of the world's international diplomacy started with the demise of the Soviet Union in 1992. All the countries under the control of the Soviet Union were liberated, and were allowed to choose their own political future. This was an era of triumphalist success of the US, and for many allied peoples across the world. Smaller countries which had previously not been well known suddenly became part of the world system. The US, with the help from Western Europe, had implemented exhaustive programmes to curb the influence of the Soviet Union and to break their authoritarian rule. It was a fight against the whole communist doctrine and the system of one - party rule by the Politburo. The US succeeded in liberating some twenty-six nations across Europe and Asia. For the first time, whole peoples could now breathe freely and live life as they chose. As part of this, each member of a family could for the first time choose whether they preferred to live life alone, independently, or collectively with family the family unit.

In the era following the collapse of the Soviet system, US intellectuals moved forward with much vigour and hard work. The thinking laid out by Thomas Paine in his seminal book of 1791, *The Rights of Man,* came under further attention as a starting point for how one justifies changes in government. In it, Paine proposes that popular political revolution is permissible when a government does not safeguard the just rights of its people. It was an argument that legitimised the revolution in France of 1798, and indeed the same thinking has been used to support countless government overthrows across the world ever since.

The treason of intellectuals did not end with the close of the Second World War. In its aftermath, subsequent generations were to live in a state of permanent war. Four national divides stand out, and have persisted for some seventy years: North Korea versus South Korea, Taiwan versus Mainland China, India versus Pakistan and Israel versus Palestinian

Why these divides are still unsettled remains a slight mystery. Was it inevitable that these binaries would run and run? Millions upon millions suffered and died in these conflicts, and the implications are far-reaching, still hounding the world with daily threats of violence. Through it all, the superpowers again are benefiting through the sale of weapons. Israel, Taiwan, and North Korea have gone ahead and developed weapons of mass destruction weapons. The world intellectual forums take great pleasure in organising debating seminars and events, to no avail. Israel has advanced so far in this course that it is now well beyond simple encroachment on territory. Palestine's capital, Jerusalem is no longer in the hands of the Palestinian people. The holy city has now become the official seat of Israel's government with control over the Al Aqsa mosque – an ancient religious centre point for millions.

The US, under the recent leadership of President, Trump, welcomed the Israeli annexations and, without hesitation, gave Israel full support to draw the map however they chose. Every day new colonies are being built in the West Bank on Palestinians territory. If it continues, Palestinians will end up in time with no option but to accept Israel's demands as a reality. President Trump was the first US president to openly support Israel, doing so apparently with pride and without hesitating in the face of widespread criticism.

In all of this, the US is favoured by its extraordinary military might – something that is without compare from any other nation. No other country can be a rival for US firepower. This gives the US the confidence to provoke dissent without worrying about consequences. They fear nobody and expressed their opinions openly without fear.

It is a great country, and when it moves in the right direction it achieves great things. Under the idiosyncratic leadership of President Trump many high calibre thinkers and politicians kept their mouths shut. Even as outrages came to be exposed in front of their eyes, they remained silent. But it should be clearly understood that President Trump was not the true face of the US. Every society may have troubled eras, where the water of political life seethes and bubbles but in time returns to still. For all that, the turbulence leaves its historical mark long after events have moved on. Hitler was not the true face of Germany, but the horrific state genocide against the Jews is something that history will never forget. Such extraordinary blips in the trajectory of a nation's history need to be clearly marked out as outlier events. They are not attached to the general background of what the country stands for.

During this period, we must look to the intelligentsia to stand firm, uncowed. In this, they have a massive responsibility. Many intellectuals rightly stood up, and condemn the president's rhetoric against Muslims. Outstanding amongst them were former President Jimmy Carter and his wife, Rosalynn. The bold support of people such as this is an essential part of the course of history and has results far down the road – often indirect and not immediately obvious, but nonetheless essential to the improvement of society in future generations.

A society grows with its roles on the basis of justice. As US President Reagan outlined in one of his speeches, the US is a country of immigrants, a melting point of many countries, and it is this very diversity that makes America great. When Europe forced almost the whole of Asia into colonial subject, it was ultimately their own downfall. In due course, the Second World War destroyed their economies and the very egos that had earlier propelled them forward in empire-building now had no option but to liberate all their colonies. Coronavirus – no less than Second World War – went on to place the entire world in mortal danger. Even vainglorious President Trump, so keen to trumpet his nation's dominance across the world, could not avoid the deadly virus. Everything happening happens for reason.

North Korea's long-standing conflict with South Korea has prevented the amalgamation of the two areas – something that is an issue with far further-reaching consequences than one might immediately imagine. US President Trump made sincere efforts to bring the two together through dialogue but the conflict remain same. Ultimately, it seems that this conflict is at least under control to the extent that it exists only as a threat to each other without actual descending into war. But the fact remains that both the countries are needlessly spending huge resources on weapons. The real beneficiary is, of course, the weapon sellers who make fools of both sides.

A similar situation exists between India and Pakistan. The original division between the two countries was made on the basis of religious dissents. There was no such issue before the English entered the continent under the name of the East India Company in 1740. When partition was being created, it was conceived by English rulers who raised the issue at a round table conference in London. They asked the recognised independent leader, Mahatma Gandhi, what form independence should take: Hindu India, Muslim India, and Princely States India. It was shocking for Mahatma, and from this point on it was clear to him that the English would not like to make India great. Large part of the Muslim population still lives in India – more than actually live in Pakistan. Kashmir, as a largely Muslim area, demands that their rulers be Muslims and consequently adopted Islamic proclamations in the state-organised system. Almost all the princely states were being ruled by Muslim rulers. Hyderabad Deccan, one of the richest Muslim states in India, was not allowed to set its own example as a separately governed region. Bengal was also divided on the basis of Muslim /Hindu. And the creation of an "East Pakistan" at distance of 1,000 miles across the other side of India was obviously never going to be workable. In due course, and inevitably, it separated in a war with India and is now known as Bangladesh.

Today both India and Pakistan pour huge resources into defence equipment at the cost of their poor communities. Instead, they should be aligned together in a fight against poverty.

Another problem is the rift between Taiwan and mainland China, both of whom have claims against each other. The US made the Taiwan issue alive through effective diplomacy and supporting infrastructural developments. When the US and

China came for a while to enjoy better bilateral relations, the issue of Taiwan waned temporarily.

Last but not least is the intractable problem of Israel and Palestinian. This is the root cause of a great many of the world's disturbances. History, going back 2,000 years, records how Christians were forever hitting at Jews as a part of their retribution for Christ's death on the cross. It is only after the Second World War that the Christian world's enmity shifted from Jews to Muslims. It was expressed through the creation of a new Israel, to be the Jewish state on Palestinian land. From positions of great power, the West was able to construct a new world order with inherent injustices that would ring through time. All the revealed books share the common notion that we should not create mischief on the earth.

The 1979 Islamic revolution of Iran follows third in a line of big peoples' revolutions that were to share the world order. The first was the Russian communist revolution of 1917, and the second was the Chinese revolution of 1949. All three were predicated on the will of the people to seize freedom – freedom of all kinds: social, economic and religious. These revolutions were against the bourgeoisie who were blamed for exploiting the poor and drawing unfairly heavy profits from their labour. The philosopher and political thinker Karl Marx (1818–1883) can be said to have laid the seeds of these populist revolts when he laid down his famous theory of Surplus Capital, articulating a source of discontentment for the masses. Many believed that it was the bourgeoisie who were the main culprit for distorting the economic rights of poor workers. In the course of such revolts, millions upon millions of innocents in the wealthier communities have been killed and their property seized and nationalized. Russia seized all the countries they occupied at the close of the Second World War and forced them under their yoke to live as communists. The US and its western allied forces were reluctant to start an all-out war with Russia, but contested what was happening through diplomatic channels, employing a carrot and stick policy. Finally, some fifty years later on 12th September, 1991, they convinced Russia that their centralised tyranny was no longer sustainable, and their communist party leader Gorbachov announced that the Soviet Union had effectively ceased to exist.

The US, now bereft of its long adversary and without war, slowly, gradually and patiently succeeded in liberating the people who had fallen under the yoke of communist rule. As a result, the peoples of the central Asian Muslim countries and of Eastern Europe, at last, had the opportunity to live their lives together alongside all the people of the world, building towards a better life.

The day to day life that the Islamic Revolution had left for the people of Iran was rather different. Religious checks were set in place to control society and monitor that it did not move out of step with what the ruling clerics perceived as the fundamental baseline of human ethics. To this day, religion has to be a central part of everyone's life, and all should follow religious ethics – something that is harshest on the female population since they must cover their head and must be careful not to display anything which might have some implication of sexual attraction. The ruling religious clerics of Iran considered Islam a model for the rest of the world, and demanded that the nation show a better ethical pattern so that people outside Iran could learn from Islam. It was not desired that the newly reinvigorated Islamic society should be influenced by the trends of the west with its open society and free-living female population. The former Shah of Iran, who once declared himself King of Kings, was considered an agent of the West.

The American CIA had sponsored a movement against the popular leader Mohammad Mosaddegh (1882–1967), who was toppled from his elected office, and ultimately died in prison. The Shah of Iran had, to his cost, disregarded Islamic principles had moved ahead too swiftly with his open modernizations plans. It was the other extreme on the spectrum compared with what was to follow once he had been deposed.

Through all of this, the West remained dissatisfied. They were frequently annoyed with the Shah of Iran, either because he suppressed his people too strongly, or because he pushed the pace of advancement too fast, threatening a standard of living that might be comparable to the western world. The failure of the Shah and the subsequent success of the Islamic Revolution are case studies in how a nation grows and adapts, for better or for worse.

The Islamic revolution of Iran draws its ethical and moral code of life from the prophet Muhammad, and Imam Ali ibn Abu Talib, first Imam and fourth Khalifa of Islam after the prophet Muhammad. Imam Ali's governance was far superior to what had gone before; he demonstrated his style of governance to such an extent that people started worshipping him, and many in mountainous regions in Syria and elsewhere – who had their doubts in accepting Jesus as a Christian symbol of God on earth – readily accepted Imam Ali as a symbol of God on the earth. Imam Ali condemned such beliefs strongly and, in many of his sermons in Kufa, spelt out that such people should be treated as infidel, Kafirs. He said, Ali is a created being and a servant to prophet Muhammad.

Imam Ali's rule was exceptionally honest, based purely on the principles of equity and justice. Religious people need to show particularly fair examples of equity and justice for the people around them. Their followers need to be persuaded by example, not by force. Equity and justice must be living examples of the rule of governance. But Imam Ali faced opposition from all corners of the newly created Islamic world. Even Ayesha, wife of the prophet, with her most close associates of the prophet, turned against him and indeed led a war against Imam Ali. She was defeated and her associates were killed. Imam Ali presented a highly conscious approach in dealing with such a difficult situation and was careful to respect the wife of the recently deceased prophet. He sent her back to Medina with honour and respect under the supervision of her brother, Muhammad bin Abu Bakar, a disciple of Imam Ali. From Syria, Muawia ibn Abu Sufyan led a big army and engaged in war with Imam Ali at Saffen. From Basra, Kharjees led another war against Imam Ali at Naharwan. Imam Ali was all time surrounded by threat, conspiracies and hypocrisy.

Iran is today facing more or less same situation that Imam Ali faced during his rule. But Iran needs to understand that US and western society will not allow any rule that stifles freedom and liberty. It was on this fundamental principle that they fought with Russia. They would not accept communist rule controlling the liberty and freedom of its people. People must be able to freely choose whatever method of life they choose to live. Accountability to God is also based on free will, not authoritarian style except civic laws. All the Abrahamic prophets avoided war with their own people. Simplicity, honesty and great goodwill with patience were their weapons. And for that reason, the world adores them even after death.

The Iran resolution was a great chance for Shia clerics to set an example of a model life pattern without killing. They failed in this, and murdered millions of their own Iranian compatriots simply on the basis that they had earlier worked for the Shah of Iran. The Prophet Muhammad's example was very clear on this when he announced forgiveness to all of his enemies who had tortured him during his mission in Mecca,

This was the prophetic way of dealing with enemies. The prophet Muhammad strictly advised his followers not to carry sword when he entered Mecca. Likewise, Imam Hussain, in the battle of Karbala, did not allow his brave brother Abnass to raise his sword. Imam Hussain took his sword out from its sheath and discarded it, and asked Abbass to go likewise without sword. If only Iran could have started their revolution with love and brotherhood for their brother Sunni Muslims, and with nobility in relations with western society. Issues like Israel versus Palestine would have been pursued through congenial diplomacy.

The Islamic revolution of Iran was unique in the history of mankind. It was led by a religious clerk, Ayatollah Khameini, aged 72. All the other big revolutions of the 20th century – Russian and Chinese – were led by militants, and they triggered wholesale massacres, to implement the change of leadership. The world, both east and west, were watching the revolution very carefully, and everyone wanted to support and help its progress. Unfortunately, the positive spirit of the revolution was mutated into something horrific. There was a huge amount of completely unnecessarily killing – Iranians killed by fellow Iranians because they had previously worked under the Shah's rule. Iranian embassies in foreign capitals poured the entire wine cellar into the gutters, and pledged to support the revolution and show the world the true spirit of Islam. Iranians under the new leadership of Ayatollah Khomeini wanted to prove that they would conduct their civil life in an exemplary fashion. The first task of Islam, showcased by the supporters of the Iranian revolution was to reflect sympathy to the poor and to demonstrate how Islam makes sure no one remains poor. Their citizens were willing to surrender surplus wealth to their needy neighbours in the spirit of the revolution. Instead, however, of following through on human reforms to show selfish motivation as intended, the revolution started on a programme of mass killings.

One of the first steps was to – quite unnecessarily – embark on direct conflict with the US. The Tehran US embassy crisis took the world by storm and shook the international community to its foundations. The initial US response had been to support the revolution because it was the will of the people. Indeed, had it followed the methodology of Islamic revolution, in line with what the prophet Muhammad demonstrated as a method of success, it might have been a moment to enlighten the world on what Islamic methods can achieve. This is Quranic message, in the event of difficulties, seeks refuge in patience and prayers. If you are truthful and on the right path, no matter how strong your enemy, by the end of the day, you will succeed. At the end of the day, the prophet Muhammad succeeded in what he was trying to do. Abu Sufyan and his commander, Khalid bin Walid, finally surrendered to the prophet, and opened the gates of Mecca for him. The prophet immediately remove the fear from the resistance of Mecca, and said "Today I trampled the hatred of man and man. All are brothers both in religion and humanity."

Fundamental to Islam are the values of peace, forgiveness, tolerance and acceptance, all these virtues which the prophet Muhammad showed at the fall of Mecca. But these were not the values followed by the Islamic Revolution of Iran, which is deeply unfortunate. Iran is an oil-rich country. If it wanted, it could have been spent on education and hospitals, not just in Iran but also across the Islamic world. The ideal scenario would have been to see Islamic universities set up under the complete sponsorship of Iran in neighbouring Muslim countries – Iraq, Pakistan, Afghanistan, Syria, Lebanon, Jerusalem. Iran missed this big opportunity. The tragedy is all the more intense because they had such a unique situation to implement such a plan;

an elderly man sitting on top just to ensure the country is not getting off track from the spirit of Islam. This elderly model of ruler is the most classical concept of the head of a family who treats all of his subjects as his children, and neighbours as brothers, and friendships and good relations to all, protecting children from enmity and ensuring they could live peacefully.

The US wanted to support the revolution, which is why the fleeing Shah of Iran was refused a visa to land in their country. But the mistakes of the revolution were too numerous to count here and the spirit of the revolution was utterly destroyed. The newly independent state embarked on war with their Islamic neighbours, which turned out to be disastrous for all involved. Even the pro-Wahabi leaders of Saudi wanted to support the revolution as long as the revolution confined itself to reforming internal society, rather than fighting the rituals of the Hajj pilgrimage and many other prayers methods.

Imam Hussain's example was exceptionally rare. It was the final manifestation of God on earth following the sacrifice of Jesus, who had risen from the dead. Imam Hussain knew what would happen to him. Jesus was tested by himself, but here Imam Hussain was tested with all his relations, where his sisters, brothers and brothers wives, cousins, children and many relations faced the worst humiliations, torture and hardship and even faced hunger and thirst. But Imam Ali did not lose his resolve even if every child, big or small, brothers and cousins suffered the most painful humiliation. Imam Ali's family were captured as war prisoners and dragged through the crowded centres of the cities, with stones thrown at the women and children. This was normal for defeated armies at this time, but if you are holding truth on your side, defeat turns out to be success. Bibi Zainab, the sister of Imam Hussain, when presented as prisoner with her family before the Islamic Khalif, Yazid ibn Muawia, told him "We have won the war forever, as long as solar systems revolve, but you have lost the war, and your name remain tarnished for all time."

What is certain is that Iran missed a great opportunity to show the meaning of success through goodwill, love and tolerance, acceptance and brotherhood. Equity and justice could have been demonstrated by spending on the poor to make them equal, starting a new era from scratch. But the opportunities were tragically missed, and instead the Iranian Revolution led to the whole region being engulfed in long-standing conflicts without outcome.

# CHAPTER IV

# Government and Governance

Government and governance, though seemingly synonymous, are differentiated by obligation and function. "Government" refers to a position, while "governance" refers to performance – in essence, how the nation's citizens are taken care of.

A military government will be one where people in government have guns, and the reality will be that an individual seeking to rise up in the organisation needs to take on duties as would be expected of a member of the military. It is, needless to say, the worst kind of government. Such a government will inevitably be peopled by sycophants – for the most part educated elites just getting by. They are willing to go along with the way things are as long they make a good living with the bonus of receiving medals and acclaim.

Military governance carries the weight of authority, and its leaders consider themselves to be great nationalists, working for the longer-term future of the country. It is a perilous route. On the way, they have learned that they have to imprison people of dissent, frequently torturing them so that they give in and accept the dictator as rightful ruler. Military dictators see the constitution as nothing more than a bunch of papers, to be torn up at any time if needs be. There are always compliant lawyers and scholars – outwardly charming and presentable to the world – whose job it is to redraft the constitution and usher in new rules, and verdicts against political opponents. The tyranny of these supporters has no limit. To see its most famous example witness how Jesus was placed on the cross by his own people. Or the betrayal of Imam Hussein by the Islamic Caliph. In contrast, western society has learnt to struggle against such military rulers, the best modern examples being France and the US.

Socialist governments have a core ethical obligation to look after the masses at large and ensure income distribution patterns that tilt towards lower and middle-class populations. This tends to come at the expense of productivity – socialist states tend to have a lower gross domestic product. The extreme of this, of course, is the communist model, as instigated by the revolutionary governments of the Soviet Union and China. Both the versions of the communist model produced drastic results in terms of their economies. In both cases, their governments were in the end brought to their knees, and both reverted back to a liberal system. However the thick blood of rule still runs in the leadership's veins and they cling on to the centralised power system that was put in place in more idealistic times, now turning it to their own ends.

The Iranian Islamic revolution was a separate and alternative model. The goal was to force the people to live life with religious practise uppermost in all they do. It is, indeed, a high and noble ambition, but unfortunately it is not something that can be imposed by force. The very leaders who set out to show the right path failed to set the good example they had anticipated and the result was that people at large became desperate to be liberated.

The monarchy is a further model for national governance, but one that is in decline. The practise of western societies has been to relegate their former monarchs to celebrity status, transferring actual power to an elected parliament.

Democracy, then, is ever and again the model that we circle back to when we debated good governance. The US President, Abraham Lincoln perhaps captured this best in his famous Gettysburg Address on 19th November, 1863 during the American Civil War.

> *"...that these dead shall not have died in vain – that this nation, under God, shall have a new birth of freedom – and that government of the people, by the people, for the people, shall not perish from the earth."*

Under such a model, there is no such thing as religious, ethnic or cultural bias in the government machinery. The goal is a free society living independently without fear of any unfair obligations or hurdles.

Whatever your walk of life, the most important thing is that one moves in the right direction, and movement in the right direction eventually results in legitimacy and, consequently, status. If the direction is not right, no matter what you do by way of reform, you will not reach the status that you aspire to. For this reason, democracy is an essential condition for better governance. If the country is not democratic in all its actions, its governance will be enfeebled. Such governments are robbed by feudal mafias, bureaucrats, the military and any other exploitative group. Rational human beings who are lovers of knowledge will fade away or be maligned by the exploiters. Such society will not be able to produce scholars, philosophers or poets of quality because intellectuals would not be able to live with self-respect in this community.

The bad old days of colonial rule did, it turns out on careful retrospective examination, do far better in this regard than one might expect. Many important thinkers emerged during the colonial period. Colonial rulers frequently had as part of their mission a goal to upgrade society and rid it of some of the more illogical inherited traditional notions. One of the first tasks for a colonial ruler was to demolish the ancient style of governance that existed locally – generally kings, their sons and the courtiers.

The first task for any civil society government is to write down its working rules of governance. The foundation of all rules-based systems must be a constitution. It is the starting point for a system whereby the laws will carry the weight of control, establishing rule without leaving it left to the subjective will of some individual or group of individuals. One very positive outcome from having this in place is the corresponding trust in the system from the people. They do not have to depend on some verbal promise but have it clearly transcribed. It is the laying down of this foundation of trust that is of prime importance.

In the end, however, even this written system is vulnerable. It depends on the upright and honest nature of those who are enforcing the written constitution. If the governing officers are not upright and cannot be trusted, no amount of written documents – formally signed and sealed – will protect the people from being cheated. Such unprincipled leaders will cheat the moment an opportunity appears before them. In the developing world, power begets power, and a circle of corrupt officials soon emerges. Those who have been made guardians of the society, to protect and nurture the nation, plunder for personal gain. As the saying goes, the foxes have been put in charge of the hen coup.

This happens in almost every developing country. The guardians break the written constitution, and, emboldened by their military uniform, happily pronounce that the new constitution is nothing more than a worthless bunch of papers, and they proudly show how these papers have been torn up and thrown away.

On this, Imam Ali's famous sermon (Nahjul Balagh: Sermon number 108) describes the situation vividly:

> *Nevertheless, now the wrong has set itself on its places and ignorance has ridden on its riding beasts. Unruliness has increased while the call for virtue is suppressed. Time has pounced upon like a devouring carnivore, and wrong is shouting like a camel after remaining silent. People have become brothers over ill-doings, have forsaken religion, are united in speaking lie but bear mutual hatred in the matter of truth*
>
> *When such is the case, the son would be a source of anger (instead of coolness of the eye to parents) and rain the cause of heat, the wicked would abound and the virtuous would diminish. The people of this time would be wolves, its rulers beasts, the middle class men gluttons and the poor (almost) dead. Truth would go down, falsehood would overflow, affection would be claimed with tongues but people would be quarrelsome at heart. Adultery would be the key to lineage while chastity would be rare and Islam would be worn overturned like the skin.*

Such societies will face hardship, and they find that everyone faces a situation where, for their own safety, they have to buy protection, and those who are without resources are left at the mercy of those who have it. Some of those who have nothing would compromise, either to become terrorists at the behest of those who control things, or to submit their honour to fall to the lowest of low. In such situations, people end up engaged in civil disobedience. Their youths become be immoral, their old men sinful, learned men turn into hypocrites and public speakers become sycophants. Such a society will cease to produce scholars, poets, philosopher or sound religious priests, and will yield only sycophants speaking nothing but lies and more lies. In such countries, society is faced with the rule of dictators. These despots suppress any rival attempts to lead, prosecuting resistors and hanging them. Dictators tend to be surrounded by sycophants, and consequently both the dictator and his sycophants consider themselves to be gifted intellectuals.

After the Second World War, western society conscientiously and very strictly followed the principles of democracy, triggered in part by the US trying to encourage it, and this brought Europe under democratic rule. No western countries ever now think it at likely they will face takeover by an army dictator. The army stands behind the scene, part of what is now described 'the establishment". It watches carefully the direction of elected leaders, monitoring and checking that it is in the spirit of national interest, and not personal interest. By contrast, in the developing world it is often the practice that elected leaders are allowed freely to rob the nation without army intervention.

The Iranian model has pre-election checked and planned beforehand. There they face religious sanctions because Iran is not liberal democracy, but it is a religious democracy. Best followed principles are to enact strong laws to check the credentials of candidates. And the spirit behind the scene is not just filling the gaps but make sure sentiments of poor uneducated people who are more than 50% in most of these countries and they are living under tribal system, that is why feudal dominates parliament. It is an old colonial style of governance, where by feudal are allowed to have easy excess to parliament, and they have controlled the parliament. Such kind of distortion always exists in the third world. Therefore, governance begins from top man, and not from bottom. It is top-down method fully recognized for its merit. Western society have gone through self-imposed discipline in life that no kith or kin, or anything that has reference of self benefits, but independent, no obligation from anybody. That is why the defeated party is not worried about any vendettas from winners. And there are strong checks and balances. Politicians are judged by their role in governance. Nepotism, favouritism and corruptions have been buried, there exist hardly any incidences where the society feels that money rules. The world bank president, appointed by President Bush as a reward for his work, was found guilty of giving extra allowance to his girl Secretary just in few months of his job, had to leave the office as an honest admission. In fact law rules. All the people are equal to laws. Nature of supreme performances bless such countries with new resources, new innovations, new technologies, and new life with prosperity and happiness. That is why western countries are flourishing with abundance's of wealth, and they spent for the farewell of their people under all the circumstances, happiness and sicknesses. Recent example of Covid-19, is an eye opener phenomenon that all people who became jobless, their governments opened the doors of their treasuries, and almost everyone was receiving from government good allowances for their better life. That is why Divine Providence keep such nations on their high status. In the third world, poor people suffered a lot due to Covid-19, that is why the whole nation faced all atrocities on their own. Such countries are hated by their own people, and also being debarred from being treated friendly. If you are not good with people, your friendly countries will become your enemies, and vice versa. Basic fundamental principles of governance are that people are not threatened by fear of spying, kidnapping, prosecuting and every fear that makes them unhappy.

Therefore, best governance depends on who is ruling. A man can be an angel, but he has to be elected not by fake votes, not by exploitation of sentiments of religion, linguistic or ethnic. It has to be done purely transparent. It is for the Security Establishment to remove weeds from politics which are appearing on sentiments and emotion. Western model of democracy is an ideal identity for parliamentary system. Establishment doesn't create hero's, there is no such thing called popularity. Man on the top must leave as soon as his term is finished. And they enjoy private intellectual life.

There is hardly any possibility that governance shows its merit without democracy. More genuine and strong democracy, more positive results will be obtained from its governance. Every living or non-living being are their responsibility, including insects, animals, forests, rivers, mountains, and human being irrespective of caste and creed. Governance of this nature see that dogs, cats, horses, cattle's and other animals are not part of street survivals, but society is responsible to look after the animals in their natural environments. If horses are kept, they are to be kept comfortable in open spaces where they can roll themselves with free breathing. Domestic animals such dogs, cats etc, are pampered and kept well in their house with full motivation of their health. Animal for slaughtering, such as cow, buffaloes, goats/sheep's and birds, all are to be protected and given full meal, and kept in hygienic conditions. It is not like in third world countries where dogs, cats are dying in the streets in hunger, diseases or die in accidents without any check. Forest and trees are bulldozed without any fear. Countries with better governance make societies responsibles for anything uncalled for.

Nature and natural conditions complement each other to facilitate human beings with a better atmosphere. The world as growing every day with new challenges, and these challenges if come across to readjust natural conditions, by moving mountains, diverting rivers, creating passages from the sea, and even from green valley, these are undertaken with the principles that such alterations are not in jeopardy with original conditions. Western societies have done wonders, by constructing Suez Canal, Hudson Bay bridge, channel-under the sea etc, all are for facilitating the growth of economy. Innovations that brings railways, motor cars and aeroplane, all these efforts are for better life. Governance positively looks after facilities that are not denied to any human being. If they succeed they move the earth, create a passage from sea, from mountains and from rivers. The world of today is greatly shaped by western societies that are motivated to innovations, discoveries and anything that makes life better for themselves and for others. Governance does not confine to status co, but to break the status co. Every day they come up with new ideas, new vision and new planning, not just waiting that someone directs them. It is both ways, the ruling party has its own plan to transform the society, and technocrats must act in cohesion with ideas impressive better, if acted upon with understanding and they together make governance to achieve better life of citizens.

And governance applications to human being must not create a class that distinguish one against other superior, all equation of services need to be designed that they act in support and not in competition. The third world is stuck up with class society which was mostly creation of colonial masters who always acted on the basis of class society. But before these countries were invaded, they were serving monarchs who by strength of their sword cease power, and frightened everyone with power of sword. Millions and millions used to be killed just to establish the authority of monarch. Tyranny used to prevail everywhere. The desire of kings can't be refused on the basis of logic. They were engaged in raising their personal holiday by undertaking huge palaces one after another, and all poor labour were sustaining their livelihood by making themselves available for the construction of palaces. No matter what best the king performs for his nations, but he is always tyrant, and must be treated as tyrant. History of mankind has passed through many crises, masses were always lying under the clutches of horses, they were being killed and their dead bodies used to be thrown openly in the arena of war and their bodies were being eaten by animals. Their women used to be taken as prisoners, slave and humiliated the way winners used to treat them. Every invader, even from the time of Alexander the Great, masses used to be forced to join the troops of invader with temptations if the war is won, women and wealth of defeated nations would be for the troops. Slowly gradually, Europe made great efforts to create a civilization by abiding laws, and laws were made by superior. Most of the things changed and improved after Second World War.

It was only after US superiority after Second World War, tried to dismental all type of class base governance, and British model bureaucracy was also moulded with new challenges. Governance must be corrected from its upper and lower base. Either top-down or bottom-up, the functionality must act smoothly between two ends and they are to make things better if working between them is in good equation and they are in harmony in their relations.

People at large are the real body of the society. Where ever people interaction is noted, it must facilitate with full priority. Society of business class, given them all leverages that made them prosper, but underlying assumptions is fully monitored that public at large is not wrong.

Good government depends upon its politician who controls the parliament. Three pillars of state: judiciary, parliament and administration, are independent. Among all functional aspects of state, judiciary is necessary to remain independent from political and parliament, best governance is found when judiciary remain watchful, both on politicians and parliament. Aristotle politics apprehended, willful act of defiance by politicians, who for popular gains compromise unlawful acts. Strong judiciary is vital for achieving justice. The third world, as it's government is rolling around politicians who made them subservient to their desires. The US and Western Europe who have long political struggles, and they found much wisdom from Greek philosophy, it was from their work who made these divisions: parliament, judiciary and administration, a position must act independent for successful government, and only through these institutions independence, rule of justice is achieved. The third world mostly lives in ancient style of government. Rulers were self-declared monarch and they continued to perpetual its influence and with time they try to turn politics into their personal dynasty.

It was only after western invasions who brought tyrant kings down, and tried to create institutional rule. Western system has such a dynamics system that it comprehends with well versed set up, distinguishing one with other based on their merits. Judges must come from qualified creed of lawyers. The laws are taught in law schools. Therefore the selection of judges is mostly on merit. Their judgements are tested and contested by lawyers who made their plead on the basis of written laws, and laws interferences. Same was also followed in administration, appointments are not on discretion of ruler, but based on written qualified examinations of civil servants. They are governed by their own rules, and if tampered with their structure, they always sought their protection from judiciary. Parliamentarians are elected by general elections.

Most of these changes were gradually implemented after Second World. Almost all the developed countries were ruled by army generals. Western society has been working hard to convert the system on democratic practises. They were faced with huge problems. At time even western countries also supported military dictators in fear of saving from the threat of overpowered communist movements. Popular vote in poor countries was easily recognized through cheap slogans against rich. A battle between politicians and military continued for more than half of the century, both systems were adopted as a compromise of accepting each other. Successful were those states, irrespective of military rule or political rule, who gave full attention to governance. Its obligations are motivated towards better services to general public.

Governance finally has its meaning of raising the society to its self sustain positions. Plato in Republic repeatedly emphasizes that it is only governance which matters. Republic definition in Plato contest is highly demanded. Best governance can be achieved under the rule of philosophers. Philosophers have better understanding on aspects that governs the society. Most important is to remove all possibilities from the ruler which makes him corrupt. Backward societies want their children should rule after their death. That is why Plato in Republic wanted that ruler should not marry because after having children his interest will be tilted to children. Ruler is the guardian of the society. How can a guardian maintain neutrality when his children interest comes in conflict with the children of the society. Mahatma Gandhi's example is popular when his child got angry with him that why he did not nominat him for going to attend barrister course in London Gandhi's wife protested that you did'nt nominate your own child Gandhi's answers to his wife that community children are also our children, and they were deserving better than our son. Therefore, good governance can only be achieved when the ruler does not distinguish children of the society from their own children. Most of the developed countries under colonial rule were well watched by their colonial masters and better performance was noted with great justice. It is only after their sovereign independence, when colonial rulers finally winded up, interest of personal rule overrides the principles of better governance.

Western society has achieved great success by adopting principles of good governance mostly from the Republic of Plato. Good governance means every item in the country must be looked after, protected and placed on its right position. Let us begin with animal life. They are at the mercy of the government. It is beyond bearable to watch how merciless society in developing countries treat animals, worst than most inhuman behaviour. Dogs, cats and several animals are living in the streets. Cattle are kept in worst form. When cattle are transported they are hanged in trucks one over other mercilessly. Forest animals are being exploited by landlords. They need to learn from western society who have kept them with love. Most of the animals are raised in open fields.

If poor children of the third world face hunger, noone feels the pinch of their hunger and they are left at the mercy of God. They have been begging either alone or with their mothers. They hardly wash their faces. Their clothes are worn out with dust. Newborn children immediately face mosquitoes, flies, lizards. In contrast, rich families have several attendance for newborn children. Rich feel pleasure to send their children to most expensive schools, yet, they stand as custodians of poor, seek their vote, look after religious rituals, sacrifices animals for poor, etc. It is only in western society where children became the focus of attention of the government.

What governance requires is that every private enterprise or government enterprise must offer best service to the society. Restaurants are checked by surprise to see if restaurants are keeping atmosphere hygienic, food is well preserved and serving in its proper hygienic conditions. Same is also followed in medical drug stores. Whereas in the third world inspectors just visit to collect envelopes for his inspection. Surprisingly, and what a details are noted, the cyclists along with drive road are protected.

Rights of men are elaborated. With small details, they prevail what is allowed to them. Rights of men are implemented with full spirit. Weaker has rights over strong. Man walking in the street has more right than man driving a car. In the third world, stronger has right over weaker. This is from where major distortion takes place.

Best model of governance is adopted by western society. Large junks of immigrants are absorbed with patience and tolerance. Every necessity is respectfully provided. Neighbours and even society at large are willing to support who are deficient to meet their needs. Basic necessities are provided at door step everywhere, they receive hygiene drinking water, tries to remove slums. Not a single Muslim country offer immigration or citizenship to foreigners though some of them are wealthy , but they are not allowed to enjoy rights of citizenship and they remain alien even though they bear same Muslim religion, same country even same language, even if they have lived there for more than 50 years children born there, married to their natives, but they are not allowed to have a citizenship. It is western system opens up immigration for everyone without biases, without sep earth rules for someone, and once they arrived as immigrants, they enjoy all rights, political, economic and social status.

Who is ruler? Western model follows strictly the path of democracy. Everything starts from the top man. If he is rightly selected by the people by popular vote through democratic system is the best way to govern. Again amazing checks. No matter how best is elected leader, but he must leave office as soon as his term is expired. Even someone serve the nation as angel, and he remained dutiful, honest exposure, yet he must leave and vacate office immediately after expiry of his office. He lives life as an ordinary man, if necessary because of security which has become threat to leaders, some sort of police surveillance is provided.

Opposed to that, the third world perpetuating its own greed of snatching, and not leaving office even after expiry, yet he would break all rules and tries to bribe judiciary and army, knowing pressure may come from there. Western world tried to establish democracy in the third world, but could not succeed, and almost every country was invaded by their own army. The growth of human values towards democracy was crushed, destroyed, even put them in ashes that never again they rise. These army generals, such as Col Ghadaffi of Libya, col Nasir of Egypt, Gen Bomedueen of Algeria, General, Turkey, Gen Suharto of Indonesia, Sadaf Hussain in Iraq, Gen Zia Ul Haq of Pakistan. Gen Marcos of Philippine, and so on almost in all Asian and South

These army generals destroyed generations over generations and ruled decades by showing humbleness, from inside they were rascals. How can country offers better governance when top men is introdders and his chosen cabinet and bureaucracy are handpicked by his greed of power. They nurtures greed over greed, nepotism, corruption was hall mark of day light robbery. Many good souls, who wanted to serve better way, washed away with time.

Slowly and gradually, US enforced democratic governments, even the neck of their leaders is under sword of army generals. US created after Second World War, a internal armed forces must watch internal and external secruity, and watch that leaders based on popular slogans may harm the country by looting the wealth of the nations.

Corruptions and nepotism are two key elements of human disease. This is a kind of disease which kills the patients. Accountability based on transparency, irrespective of any notions that retains inner demise of own interpretation against opponents, would be greeted as killing patient mercilessly. Corrupt officers checking corruption of other officers is like a dragging human ego to its false kings, and they face doom days together. Across the board, no matter what affiliation one belongs, or one involved helping dirty acts of killing innocent leaders are absolved from corrupt because of inner circle monitors corruption as a political tool, and not in national interest. In such countries, judges are installed to fulfil their procedures in return of their appointments, and they also do the same thing. Western society has strange culture, daughters witnessing against fathers, while doing so, they cry at the crime of their father, but not to hide the truth. Lies is the biggest crime in western society. Anything based on fake information would be charged under the act of cheating. These societies are moving ahead with happiness for all its residents, and they live happily without any fear from any of its citizens. Laws are very clear, and police acts as protector of the victim. Everything comes from top man. If he acts correctly, make himself responsible for any act wrongfully commuted.

First and foremost task of governance is to ensure that all human beings are equal in laws. And among all necessities, the most result-oriented philosophy is to upgrade the society from its bottom to its highest level of better and protected life for all of its citizens. Income distributions must set in such a way that income level gaps are minimized. There should be no body to be defined as personal servant. Human beings may be given dignity. If someone is engaged for personal attendant, then owner must contribute health insurance, pensions contributions as adopted in western countries. Personal servants are not to be treated as slave. They are not beaten, insulted or abused. If landlords engage poor farmer for his agriculture farm, then the education of farmer's children, their health must be born by owner by same criteria as per facilities are extended to industrial labour.

Such society is always in state of emergency all the time, and continue to maintain struggle against tyranny, who has no clue of governance but only knows how to win by hook and crook, and bulldoze whatever come in front of him. Society is destroyed by tyrant by keeping them as their subservient, many scholarly personalities give up their ego, and drop down their pen before tyrant. The third world must learn from western society how they keep their principles and conscience alive even in difficult times. Unfortunately, western countries sometimes in their own interest turn their deaf ears and get along with tyrant to achieve their own goal. The US being a global leader, over looking everywhere, sometimes allows tyrants military leaders are allowed to seize power, and kill as many as he can, because something higher valueable goals are to be achieved, and Supremacy of democracy is compromised. Emotional democracy has no valuation, as it is achieved based on sentiments of poor people who have no vision but to their limitations with own boundaries. The third world has emotional problems. Many analyst failed to answer when democracy is working very well in India, which is unique example. India is not an homogenous society, there are many nationalities, regional dimensions, religious distinguishing, linguistic, closure and caste, all are at variance, yet democracy prevails in its roots, and that is why India such a large populated society with its long borders all around the mountain and occasions, sustain independent sovereign nation.

Poverty, abject poverty that people suffer in the third world is something that one can conceive that people with such a wide disparity, one side may be 5% living luxurious life, 20%, living gracefully, described as middle class, rest of 75% living life as human cattle, and the rest of world have closed their eyes, and they are just engaged in their day to day affairs for their own prosperity. It is a massive crime if poor are left merciless without being mentioned about them. Divine retribution strikes at appropriate time, and unknown egoistic living in fake self-conceived ideas of their own ultimately suffer. Prosperity of all countries depends upon their rule of justice, which envisages that rulers must not turn deaf ears to the plight of poor masses. The US and western countries not just to look after those who suffer absolute poverty in their own countries, but they are the one who even go to most poverty horizon countries like Africa. In Africa, US in collaboration with western countries, have undertaken wonderful and miraculous jobs of getting most remote forest inhabitants, even many not exposed to civility are now being dragged out from unhygienic ditches and now living relatively better. History witnesses many empires, richness, and high moral societies but finally washed away by atrocities appearing different forms, wars internal, external, and worst is pandemic. The west struggled against slavery and finally eliminated from its roots. Not just salivary, personal servants most popular in the third word, rich people enjoying high level of royal and comfortable life on the plight of poor masses. In rural area, feudal land lords rule. Poor peasants are living most horrible life under the supervision of their feudal land lords. They command , and snatch their historical right of vote. These peasants are taken in trucks at polling stations. Nearly 70% people in the third world live in country side. So the winner of popular vote goes to feudal landlord, and they form majority in so called democracy of the third world. Good governance must show its credibility that ruling party should not exercise its influence in election. Western model is always there.

Good governance means people in the state are not pushed to gutters where people without houses makes their houses on guttering in area which are mostly unhygienic. Ruling system if based on liberal democracy, it has in it, a built in mechanism that representative of the parliament are bound to answer and they look after their constituencies with whatever efforts, it give people little respect that someone always return for their help.

# CHAPTER V

# Free Will & Liberty

The rule of Justice is a basic and fundamental principle of life. All religions, irrespective of the differences that may exist between them, or whether they accept or reject the principles upon which they are built, concur on the fundamental principle that Justice lies at the heart of any code for civilised existence.

In the rivalry that has always existed between competing faiths, much hatred has often been generated, with further heat from the commentaries and rhetoric. But the fundamental truth that always survives is that each human being needs to find their own the means to live without hurting others – an ethical course which ensures them personal integrity.

The three great Abrahamic faiths, each with their own prophet, acknowledge God, the Almighty, the single creator of all. Where they differ is in their beliefs surrounding the afterlife. The Jews, Christians and Muslims all bury their dead. They do so in the belief that the spirits of their loved ones will be raised again for the Day of Judgement. Those who choose to cremate their dead, do so in the separate belief in a rebirth that will reflect the deeds of the deceased – a concept that is, in many ways, related to the concept of transmigration.

## In the Beginning…

Creation itself remains the biggest mystery of them all. Of the world's ancient prehistory we have few concrete traces, and that very first initial act of creation remains one of the biggest mysteries of all. How and when our universe appeared remains shrouded in mystery. Surely those enormous heavenly bodies with all their scarcely understood effects on our earthly world must be signs of someone out there who has created this universe? The rotation of day and night is one such miracle with that wonderful symmetry and rhythm. The very winter and summer are governed by a host of planetary systems. The unknowable ancient creation history of the universe is given to us only through what is revealed in divine books. These books come to us as related by the people who have been chosen to do so by the Creator – our prophets.

One widely accepted interpretation of our history is that the Earth was alive long before the arrival of human beings. What can be known of that first creation? The great ancient philosophers of Greece, Plato, Aristotle and Socrates repeat ever and again that nothing is created by itself. There must be, therefore, a Creator. Who might have created that initial creator is a question that remains unanswered. On this basis, the philosophers concur that God is it once created and uncreated.

Such paradoxes are around us everywhere. For example, the definition of the beauty all around us eludes us in the same way. It is beyond our abilities to know how such marvellous creatures can exist and we and marvel at the bright colours, and the amazing forms, and at the remarkable intellect of the animals that surround us. The miraculous balance of the ecological world is a similar miracle – the levels of complexity and subtlety are surely evidence of an all-powerful Creator. Similarly, scientists exploring the great extent of our solar system find have not yet reached 10% of its great design. Our prophets, who have revealed so much to us in their books, explain a lot of this for us. They confirm the directions that the planets move in, and the rotations they follow, and they give some insight into the building blocks of our immense solar system.

But through all of this, the biggest question which still haunts most philosophers is 'For what purpose was all of this conceived and created?' And why would the humble human sit at the heart of all of this, only to be washed away when he meets his death? This itself remains another eternal question. To what purpose is our life it can be terminated at any time, and if we might finish it as if never born? The revealed books give us some guidance through this complex maze, and tell us something of the remarkable story of the creation of man and our ultimate purpose.

From them, we learn that God created man. He created Adam in the heavens, and he asked the angels to fall to their knees in prostration as he blew the spirit of life into Adam's form. All of them accordingly obeyed the command of God. All, that is, except one: Iblis. He was later to carry other names – Satan, or the Devil, or a Demon, amongst others. All of these names are centred in the one being who seeks to draw man off the rightful path, the path shown by God.

Adam lived at first contentedly in heaven, but under the solemn warning that he was not to go anywhere near the holy tree, which would cause him harm. The Devil, however, was keen to prove that this new man – the creation of God – could be easily tempted, and that man would be vulnerable to greed. He was successful. Adam was diverted from his course and went to the prohibited tree to pluck that first apple. From this God took a lesson and decided that habitation in heaven would be a gift only bestowed upon those who succeeded in overcoming similar trials set before them down on Earth – a kind of obstacle course. To this end, Adam was sent down from heaven to earth. He was told that he would be there for a limited time, and that he would, in the end, face all the consequences of his deeds, good and bad. It was made clear to him that his return to heaven would depend on these deeds.

In time, God conveyed further instructions, carried to man through his chosen prophets. "Follow these instructions," these prophets told us, "and your trials will be limited." It is from this starting point that the story of a man on Earth begins. Free will is a choice given to human beings at the outset. Do what you like, and each of us will be responsible for our own needs. Whether you are good or you are bad, whether you are just, or unjust, all these outcomes lie within your own hands. What is "Just" is defined by your rights, and what is given to you. What is "Unjust" is that with does not belong to you, the belongings of somebody else. If you steal from others things which are not yours, you will be committing an unjust act.

## Justice and Free Will

However what is Just and what is Unjust is not always straightforward, and around this there can often be much discussion. We must try to follow a few basic principles, and be wary of missionaries who convey distorted interpretations of what is right. To kill someone without any reason must surely be Unjust. But to kill someone with a good reason, possibly in defence when under threat, may be Just. The judgement in such cases is complex and can be highly subjective. Underpinning the deed is the question of motivation. Motivation, in this context, has its own meaning. Here we mean a purpose that is to the benefit of all and not simply for one person. An undisputed Just motivation would be to fight against an occupying force. The occupier, by having taken land, is Unjust. In this case it is for the common good that we should fight the occupier.

At the heart of the role of justice lies of the concept of free will. The role of monks and other such religious figures is an interesting one in this context. They impose upon themselves religious sanctions, effectively surrendering their free will and removing from themselves the temptations that God has laid down to test man. Such religious figures are often highly venerated and their views sought in relation to deciding what is just or unjust. But the principles which they are living by are fundamentally against the rule of liberty and freedom for all. Liberated people are those who are free to make their own decisions. These decisions might be motivated by religious ideas or cultural values or indeed, tribal principles. With so much pressure upon the individual it can be hard to make the right decisions. Sadly, most of the developing world lives in this state, oppressed by tribal elders who strip them of their free will and remove the liberty.

## The Tyranny of Leaders
In this environment, those who are happiest are the ones who live contentedly within their own small circle. Their options are curtailed because they are economically dependent. They live under the influence of a patriarchal man – yes, it is always a man – who controls the economic well-being of the tribe. In such a patriarchal unit, one man receives a share from all that is earned from the agricultural land – sometimes as much as 95%. Often the leader will claim to be some sort of religious figure. The reality is that they are no more than a criminal or tyrant. In such societies religious figures place themselves above the common people and shroud themselves in mysterious authority.

Truly religious societies will be clear that no person is inferior to any other either in terms of human dignity or earnings. The wealth of individuals must be the wealth of nations and is not for personal use. A test of this can be seen from those who share their wealth and donate generously to public institutions. In reality there are very few who share in this way. For the most part religious leaders in these communities in the developing world are creating wealth for their own children. Great are those nations where such personal greed does not play a role – the societies of the western world where we see people spend billions upon billions of dollars to the benefit of their society. They shoulder a share of the government's duty to care for the people, and in these societies the money spent by private donors far exceeds what even the government disperses. The world's best universities and hospitals are created by private groups who fund these institutions as part of their social contribution for the greater good of the people.

The concept of a nation state is closely allied to a desire create good for all in the community. The concept of such a state goes back to the beginnings of time and the very earliest human community is. It is a subject which the philosopher Jean-Jacques Rousseau (1712–1778) explores, and he describes how collective living together provides the motivation to build something and defend the community from intruders who have not opted for this plan to develop the common good. This is the resistance of a highly civilised social unit rebuffing the attacks of those seeking immediate personal gratification by force. Man was born free but has been chained by himself, an option consciously chosen to protect himself from the others.

Is it the same for the rest of God's creatures on this earth? Yes, indeed. To some degree it is the law of the jungle that every big animal eats the smaller animals. However, among the animals there is no such system of self organisation for the common good. They live in complete freedom, with all the bad stuff that comes along with such liberty – the inability to work as a group in self-defence and the consequent vulnerability to attack in a "dog eat dog" world. They lack the intellectual capacity to build a community for the common good. In this sense, man is a very special creature, for whom whole vast vistas are opened up as a result of his intellectual ability. Man, with his great intelligence, straddles the Earth, criss-crossing the oceans and creating passages across the seas, moving mountains and carving up landscapes. Such ventures have only been possible as a result of grouping together for the common good. In time, however, such groupings have themselves mutated all too often into forces for injustice, seeking to enslave their own people, or to conquer those around them. Communities have grown into whole new nations, which in time have grown further and sought dominance the one over the other. Wars have resulted. In such contests it is the weak who suffer most. Tragically, it is the women of this earth who are most vulnerable and suffer most in such wars. For this alone it is beholden on us all to find improved systems of governance and make our communities live stronger together and more safely.

## Plato's Republic

The Greek philosopher Plato, in his book, *The Republic*, has delved deeply into the principles of justice, stating that they function as the soul in the body state. In Plato's terms the State can be seen as a body, and its governance, its soul. If the soul becomes infected, then it is the whole body that will suffer as a result. A state which has not succeeded in liberating itself from national taboos will never be successful. Such societies, where patriarchs look only to the safeguarding of their own children's futures, and do so by devouring the wealth of all around them, inflict suffering on all.

Plato points out that a ruler typically sees himself as a guardian and his interpretation of justice is to look after his own children and relatives. The result is that he will try to install his own kith and kin in positions of power and authority. The selection of a ruler is, then, of paramount importance. Identifying the right individual – one who has high moral values and competence – can never be straightforward. In the developing world this goes astray all too often. The connivance of thugs, cooperating together to manipulate their control, manages to make a mockery of democratic practises. If the ruler at the centre of government is corrupt, that corruption will roll out through the entire society. If he is a tyrant, all will live under his threat. If the ruler is illiterate, or under-educated, he will in turn produce a society where the masses are also illiterate. It is for these reasons that Plato emphasised that the ruler needs also to be a philosopher-king. Only then can the ruler ensure the right balance of fair play and justice. He must be resilient to the corruption of those closest to him, be they even his dearest friends and relatives, and he must be prepared to impose punishments upon them if necessary. Imam Ali, when he was Caliph, was one such a leader. As ruler of the Islamic world he was strong even in the face of the anger of his brothers. A religious leader needs to enforce the code of that religion, and show himself at the same time to be humble, setting vivid examples for the welfare of the society.

Religion and free will are God's gifts to man – a code given to human beings to live and create their own path to happiness. God, all-powerful and omniscient, could have chosen to make the world follow one single religion. But to do so would have reduced man's individual sense of accountability and stripped him of his choice and his ability to act freely. So what, then, is the role of the state and indeed how did the state first come into existence in the first place? Should states be bound by religious laws? These are all vital areas that need further investigation, a subject of debate through the ages.

## Religious Man and Civic Man

There are additional duties born by religious figures. More than their secular counterparts, they are bound to be honest, compassionate, patient, sympathetic to sufferers, and to live within their means. They must not create hurdles for other believers who also want to be religious figures in the group. Their actions must be carried up with peace and tranquillity at all times. Above all it was shown that anything that instigates hatred between the people, does so for all our children of God, and ultimately it is He who he will judge what is right and what is wrong. An earthly leader will be outstanding, superior to the others, if his conduct is clearly seem to be upright, and his treatment of others is tolerant and compassionate, and if he ignores those who seek to hurt him.

One of the most important duties of a religious leader is to develop a relationship with the creator. Each of the Abrahamic faiths moves in its own direction, and it can only be the Creator who will know what is ultimately right. Such knowledge, as Plato points out, is denied to us human beings. But these prophets, who came after Plato, did something to shed some light. Ultimately, the people of the book – the Jews, Christians and Muslims – all follow the same God and have a code for day-to-day life that does not conflict between them. These codes cover so much: what are the best eating habits, what should not be eaten, how relations should be between men and women, how marriages should be conducted, and the rights of each parent over their children. Other broader points are also covered: what should be done with surplus wealth, and how to dispose of the bodies of the deceased in readiness for the day of judgement. Outside the central faiths there are other beliefs systems and their behaviour often transgresses these codes. Their followers eat dogs, snakes, horses, donkeys, monkeys and indeed anything that they wish. The Hindus for example, choose to place the dead man in a fire and burn the remains, and there are reports in recent times of Hindus drinking cow urine to ward off coronavirus.

The concept of an overarching secular state originally came into existence as a way to protect the rights of each citizen, irrespective of cast creed or religion. Religious figures bear the burden of society alongside the secular civilians – they live in harmony and they follow the same civic responsibilities so that they can live in peace with each other. Each share the responsibility of looking after the welfare of their society. One thing that they will always have in common is esteem for the importance of Justice. In a secular state, the individual citizens wander free, able to do whatever they want, and removed from the coercion of family, father, mother, children. The state protects them as individuals, and make sure that they are not unjustly be treated. There has to be harmony between the secular state and the religious codes that people live by, but nothing must be done that puts in danger the individual's right for free will.

In all of this the religious man stands by his central belief that the commander of the entire universe is the Creator. Each person's destiny is under the creator's hand. There is no harm in anyone seeking refuge in the creator, and, as a result, feeling protected and cared for. From this his self assurance and happiness can grow strong. For large numbers of people religion plays this central role in their lives, and it becomes an essential part of their identity, while living free from the more controlling aspects of a faith system. Jews and Christians have given a great deal of care and attention to the study of the role of the state, and as a result they have improved the welfare systems, ensuring that the individual is looked after. Western societies, particularly the United States, have created environments where humanity prospers and have fostered communities where all can study and undertake research to gain a deeper understanding of the universe and how it works. Central to all of this is the vital role of education. In these societies, education is freely available and there is respect and esteem for people who can show themselves to be learned and clever. For them career opportunities arise as a consequence. Working together, research and development projects explore additional ways to improve society. The results have been remarkable. Through all of this, these societies maintain high levels of religious tolerance, respecting the beliefs of others. This emancipated world is very different from the rather closed traditional societies in the developing world, where religion enforces countless bottlenecks, stifling creativity and suffocating freedom of thought. In such communities religion becomes a straitjacket, narrowing the vision.

In these open, cosmopolitan western societies people do not make a judgement call on one another based on religious beliefs. Nor is religion ever compulsory. Everyone is free to follow whatever path they choose, by respecting other beliefs of others. People from different religious systems inter-marry, and the children that result are faced with their own choices in selecting the faith that they will follow. As Plato pointed out, a society is stronger if the young take their identity from a sense of nation rather than a sense of tribal name. Any identity which is not collective and is actually tied back only to a family unit is a society in which the network nodes are not as well-connected and it cannot grow effectively. Such societies still exist all over the world, following small insular tribal systems. These societies tend to impose enormous inhibitions upon the individuals. In contrast, western societies tend to move forward from this point and as a result the collective group evolves, providing a more open system that stimulates scientific and technological innovation. The individuals are working together and cooperating, rather than looking back to smaller units based on family names. The inhabitants of traditional villages in the developing world, where cast and creed are essential symbols that the people regard is their essence, end up unfulfilled – seeds that germinate but fail to grow.

Both of the societies – the emancipated cosmopolitan world of the west, and the more inward looking traditional societies of the developing world – keep religion pretty much in name only. They follow the rituals and live by some of the important symbols, and their lives are punctuated by the religious calendar. Islam places a strong emphasis on equality and fairness, but this is sadly not respected in most places. More than 50% of the population in most Muslim societies live in absolute poverty. Failure to achieve equality and justice leads to sectarian differences and further disputes. The societies become a rich pickings for military dictatorship – societies that suffer horrendously at the hands of the liars and hypocrites have taken control of the governmental organisation.

It is heartening perhaps to look back at the European states who were, many of them, before the Second World War, also under some form of authoritarian rule or even military dictatorship. Portugal under Salazar, Spain under Franco, Italy under Mussolini, Germany under Hitler, Czechoslovakia under Tito, and most of Eastern Europe managed by puppet quislings whose strings were controlled from Moscow. These societies were ultimately successful at liberating themselves from these constraints – events that happened in recent history. The developing world continues to find it hard to follow the same course. Military rule seems to have become very much part of the fabric of day to day expectations. Old feuds die hard, and disputes fester between nations, ultimately holding them back from the development work they should be focusing on.

Saddled by relentless dictators who bleed the country dry, these societies suffer immensely. There people are born into slavery and their prospects are miserable. They will receive propaganda to persuade them that the system is working better than the democracies in the west, but it is a manoeuvred presentation used by the corrupt elite to maintain their way of life. After the Second World War, the European countries were successful in moving to a democratic system and managed to throw off the shackles of their dictatorships. One by one Portugal, Spain, Italy and Germany started afresh, and the Eastern European countries were also eventually liberated from the Soviet Union which had held them so long in its grip.

The success of these western societies is deeply embedded in the fact that their people adhere conscientiously to the principles of democracy at all levels of political life. The fundamental rule is that no one has the right to lead the country except by consensus. The honesty of that consensus is guaranteed by the secret ballot.

To quote the famous words of Abraham Lincoln (US President 1861–1865): "Government of the people, by the people, for the people, shall not perish from the Earth."

# AFTERWORD

The recent Covid-19 pandemic has engulfed the entire world, from east to west and from north to south. No country is safe from its life threatening influences. More than one million people have already died and many more are doubtless not reported.

This kind of pandemic does not appear by itself. There is always a reason. When society faces good or bad events, it generally means something has gone wrong somewhere. Its root lines in some human error or deeds. Divine Providence is always in force. At times it turns a blind eye to human tyranny and the errant behaviour of tyrants. It does so, in order to leave room for other human beings to bring influence to bear and drive through reform. Such is the nature or free will left to us from on high.

But if tyrannical behaviour crosses certain limits, Divine Providence swings into action. It is not always just the tyrant leader who is punished; sometimes it is the whole society that suffers a collective punishment. The revealed books describe this phenomenon, and show how a whole society will suffer alongside its tyrant ruler because they did not fight against the tyrant and they simply accepted him.

One should not fear death if one's efforts are honest, taken with the  greater good of society in mind. For this, there is always reward - possibly not in your own lifetime, but maybe in that of your progeny who will benefit in time. The details and the workings of this divine mechanism are something about which no one has knowledge.  These societies often receive their reward far down the line, passed down by ancestors who gave generously with the greater interest of that society in mind.

It is a strange coincidence that Covid-19 has appeared exactly 100 years after the Spanish flu pandemic of 1918. The Spanish flu killed millions in that era. It came at a time of international upheaval. The horrors of the First World War had just come to a close, and in Russia the communist revolution was paving the way for the long repression of the Soviet regime. The Great Depression followed soon, laying waste to the post war optimism of the roaring 20s. The whole period ushered in a new age where Europe and Russia tussled over land and power, ever anxious that the balance of control might some time swing unequivocally one way or the other.

The average European is probably not deeply bothered about political rule, but they are disturbed about political unrest and society instability. Such a period may now be across the horizon again.

Covid 19 has shattered lives for so many people who were living well. It is a retribution for wrongdoings. Worst hit is the US, followed by Europe. In the great scheme of things, society now has to pay back for the harm done to others.

President Trump's actions at this time were unusual. No other American President taken liberties with his personal control in this way. He had, in effect, created his own definition of the

Rule of Justice. Many people inside US, and many outside were under threat of being destroyed by the new world order that President Trump was seeking to establish.

Since he left office, the situation has been improving. There was a collective sigh of relief in the whole world. The US was able to demonstrate that it was a true democracy, and the undemocratic aspirations of their President were dispatched and quashed. In statistical sampling, if some data is not consistent with the rest, these elements are removed from the sample - they are the "outliers". Trump, in the same way, was not a standard American sample. US society, which has its core values, recognised him as an outlier and voted in President Biden in his place. Biden's advanced years - at 78 years old he is the oldest US president to have been sworn in - were not judged a sufficient obstacle to bar him from the essential role of replacing his predecessor. The choice was a democratic one, and re-established order and ethical rule.

It seems that President Trump was trying to imitate the Russian and Chinese models - holding on to power up until death. To achieve this, he attempted to get the collaboration of US army generals. He underestimated the education levels of US society. All of the army generals had signed their mandate confirming that they to stood unalterably behind the constitution. In many countries in the developing world, Generals not only jump to seize power but also create the power vacuum in readiness for army control. Such countries, where the army monitors its own citizens with guns, are far from just, and its citizens are ever under threat – aside from those who are supporters of army rule for their own personal interests. America showed itself, that day, to be safe from such corruptions.

Humanity can grow only in countries who hold the flag of Liberty and Freedom by their side. There is a natural cycle to the system of democratic rule. The beauty of the political system is that it rotates and is not confined to one man. The poisonous attitudes which infect a ruler over time lead, in the end, to the ruler's loss of elected office. A fresh political environment is ushered in with the new political team, like new water to the crop. The political rotation through the democratic system regenerates energy, whatever crisis the countries faces.

This rotation of faces is wonderful medicine, keeping a good democratic system alive and well.